Japanese College Students' Motivation for Reading English

Japanese College Students' Motivation for Reading English

Chiyo HAYASHI

KEISUISHA

Note on author
Chiyo Hayashi, Ed. D
Professor at Kunitachi College of Music
Master of Arts from Eastern Michigan University (Major: English and American Literature)
Doctor of Education from Temple University (Major: Applied Linguistics)
Research Interests: Individual differences in second language learning (motivation and beliefs), pronunciation, and curriculum development

【著者】林　千代
現職：国立音楽大学音楽学部　教授
略歴：イースタンミシガン大学英米文学学部修士課程修了。テンプル大学教育学部応用言語学博士
　　　課程修了。国際基督教大学専任講師を経て、現職。
専門：応用言語学、英語教育学（特に学習者要因に関する研究）

Copyright©2018 Chiyo Hayashi
Printed in JAPAN

ALL RIGHT RESERVED. No part of this work may be reproduced,redistributed, or used in any form or by any means without prior witten permission of the publisher and copy-right owner.

Published by **KEISUISHA co., ltd.**
1-4 Komachi Naka-ku Hiroshima 730-0041 Japan

ISBN978-4-86327-431-0 C3082

本書は国立音楽大学による平成 29 年度出版助成を受けています。

まえがき

　本書は、著者が行った「日本人大学生の英語リーディングに対するモチベーション」研究に基づくものです。この研究は、「英語学習者の読解力を向上させるのにはどうしたらよいのだろう」という素朴な疑問からスタートしました。近年の第二言語（以後L2）におけるリーディング研究では、読解のプロセスにおいて、様々な認知的な要因（例：ワーキングメモリー、語彙認知力、背景知識など）が重要な役割を果たすことが明らかになっています。最近では、認知・メタ認知ストラテジーがリーディングのプロセスに果たす役割が解明され、リーディング・ストラテジーが読解指導に広く取り入れられるようになりました。しかし、現状では、依然として、読解指導を訳読式に頼る教員も多く、どのように効果的にリーディングの指導を行うか、悩んでいる教員も少なくありません。特に、英語を苦手とする学習者の読解指導は、教員の大きな課題となっています。筆者はこのような学生を指導するうちに、上記に記した認知的な要因以外にも着目する必要があるのでは、と強く思うようになりました。また、読解の指導法としては、一つのアプローチに頼るだけではなく、いくつかの指導法を包括的に統合した授業を行うことが効果的である、とも考えるようになりました。そこで着目したのが第一言語（以後L1）におけるリーディング・モチベーション研究です。

　1990年代半ばから、アメリカにおいて、L1学習者の「リーディングに対する情意面」に関する研究が盛んに行われてきました。米国の子供たちの深刻な読書離れに端を発するこの研究は、リーディングのスペシャリストであるJohn Guthrie教授（University of Maryland）と教育心理学の専門家であるAlan Wigfield教授（University of Maryland）が中心

となって、始まりました。近年の教育心理学における「モチベーション理論」の知見に基づいて、「学習者のモチベーションはアカデミックな領域によって異なる(domain-specificity of motivation)」という前提のもとに進められた多くの実証研究の結果、1）リーディング・モチベーションは内発的・外発的モチベーションなどの複数の心理的要因から成り立っており、2）読解力とモチベーションには有意な相関関係があり、3）内発的モチベーションを高めることにより、読書量が増え、その結果、読解力が高まる、ということが実証されました。これらの結果に基づいて、認知面と情意面の両方に焦点をあてた「教科取り入れ方読解指導法」、Concept Oriented Reading Instruction（以後 CORI）が構築されました。現在、CORI はアメリカの小・中・高・大学生を対象に実施され、多くの教育機関で成功を収めています。

　本研究では、上記のＬ１リーディング・モチベーション研究成果を基に、日本人大学生の第二言語である英語でのリーディングに対するモチベーションを調査しました。横断研究としてアンケート調査を行い、統計分析を行い、その結果として明らかになったのは、「内発的なモチベーション」が英語でのリーディングに最も重要な役割を果たしており、その次に、英語に対する「道具的動機」が影響を及ぼしているという結果でした。また、モチベーションを予測する要因としては、「英語リーディングに対する自信」が大きな影響力を持つこと、しかし、「日本語での読書好き」は必ずしも「英語での読書好き」にはつながらないことも明らかになりました。

　本研究の結果が示しているのは、英語でのリーディング・モチベーションにおける「内発的動機」と「自信」の重要性です。つまり、「読むのが面白い、楽しい」と「内容がわかる、理解できる」という２つの側面を織り込んだ読解指導を行うことで、英語を読むことへのモチベーションが高まることを示唆しています。英語を非常に苦手とし、英語を読むことを苦痛に思う学生でも、理解できるインプット、

まえがき

　興味深く共感を呼ぶ内容を読むことで、「英語を読むことが楽しい」と感じ、「もっと英語の本が読みたい」と思うようになる可能性も示しているように思います。本研究の成果を踏まえて、今後、学習者がもっと英語が読みたいと自発的に思い、その結果として、読書量が増え、読解力も高まる「L2リーディングの授業モデル」を構築したいと考えています。

　本書は、テンプル大学博士課程に提出した博士論文を若干の加筆と修正を行ったものです。本研究を進めるにあたって、多くの方のご指導とご協力をいただきました。テンプル大学博士課程の指導教官としてご指導していただいた David Beglar 先生、Jim Elwood 先生、アンケート調査に協力していただいた先生方・学生に心から感謝の気持ちを述べさせていただきます。また、長期に亘る研究と執筆を温かく支えてくれた家族に、この場を借りて、感謝の気持ちを伝えさせていただきます。最後になりましたが、本書の出版をお引き受けいただき、刊行にご尽力いただいた渓水社の木村斉子氏に、心からお礼を述べさせていただきます。

　なお、本研究は、文部科学省科学研究費補助金（平成 22～24 年）を受けて進められました。

2018 年 1 月 31 日

Table of Contents

まえがき i

The Study

CHAPTER 1 INTRODUCTION
The Background of the Issue 3
Statement of the Problem 5
Purposes and Significance of the Study... 7
Theoretical Perspectives 8
The Organization of the Book 9

CHAPTER 2 REVIEW OF THE LITERATURE
Motivation Defined 11
Theories of Motivation Applied to the L1 Reading Doman 13
    Expectancy-Value Theory 13
    Self-Efficacy Theory 15
    Self-Determination Theory 17
Research on Motivation for L1 Reading 24
    The Background of the Research on L1 Reading Motivation 25
    Reading Motivation Defined 25
    Components of L1 Reading Motivation 26
    The Development of the Motivation for Reading
    Questionnaire 27
    The Relationship Between Reading Motivation and Reading
    Performance 29
    Children's Reading Motivation, Reading Amount, and Text
    Comprehension 29

Summary of L1 Reading Motivation Research 32

CHAPTER 3 L2 READING MOTIVATION RESEARH

Research on Motivation for L2 Reading 35

Summary of L2 Reading Motivation Research 41

The Gaps in the Literature 42

Purposes of the Study and Research Questions 44

CHAPTER 4 METHODS

Participants 45

Instrumentation 47

    The Reading Motivation Questionnaire 47

Procedures 49

Analysis 50

Chapter Summary 51

CHAPTER 5 COMPONENTS OF L2 READING MOTIVATION

Results 53

The Relationships among the Factors 59

Discussion 60

    Intrinsic and Extrinsic Motivations for L2 Reading 61

    Intrinsic Motivation for L2 Reading 61

        L2 Intrinsic 62

        Desire to Read 62

    Extrinsic Motivation for L2 Reading 63

        Instrumental 63

        Importance 64

        Recognition 65

        Compliance 66

        L2 Specific Factors 67

Summary of the Findings 67

CHAPTER 6 L2 READING MOTIVATION MODEL

      L2 Reading Motivation Model 69
            Creating the L2 Reading Motivation Model 69
            Results 70
            Discussion 72
      Chapter Summary 75

CHAPTER 7   PEDAGOGICAL IMPLICATIONS
      Fostering Intrinsic Motivation for L2 Reading 77
      Instrumental Orientation for L2 Reading 78
      Self-Confidence in L2 Reading Ability 79
      Content-Based Reading Instruction for L2 Classrooms 80
      Concept Oriented Reading Instruction 81
      Chapter Summary 82

CHAPTER 8   CONCLUSION
      Summary of the Findings 83
      Limitations 84
      Suggestions for Future Research 85
      Final Conclusion 86

REFERENCES 87
APPENDIXES 97
      The Final L2 Reading Motivation Questionnaire (Japanese) 97
      The Final L2 Reading Motivation Questionnaire (English) 99

Japanese College Students' Motivation for Reading English

CHAPTER 1
INTRODUCTION

The Background of the Issue

With the advent of the digital age, the amount of information people are exposed to has increased drastically. To keep up, people are obliged to read a wide variety of both digital and paper texts including newspapers, magazines, books, documents, instructions, and advertisements. Consequently, the ability to read efficiently and with high levels of comprehension has become an even more crucial skill for success and achievement in many aspects of modern life.

Numerous researchers and educators have acknowledged this central role for reading in the modern world and many have investigated predictors of growth in reading comprehension. Considerable research has been conducted on cognitive aspects of reading, such as orthographic decoding, memory, schemata, and lexical and syntactic knowledge. In recent years, however, first language (L1) reading specialists and educational psychologists have also shed light on affective aspects of reading, in particular, motivation for reading. They have proposed that because reading is an inherently effortful activity that requires focused attention and concentration, affective variables will significantly influence reading processes.

Accordingly, during the last decade, much research has been conducted on first language (L1) readers' motivation for reading. The findings have consistently demonstrated the multifaceted nature of such motivation: it is not a unitary construct but consists of several affective variables, including intrinsic motivation, extrinsic motivation, and reading efficacy (Baker & Wigfield, 1999; Wigfield, 2000; Wigfield & Guthrie, 1995, 1997; Wigfield, Guthrie, & McGrough, 1996).

Further, researchers have shown that motivation and reading performance are closely related (Guthrie, 2001; Guthrie & Davis, 2003; Guthrie et al., 2006; Torgesen et al., 2007). For example, a study conducted by Guthrie, Wigfield, Metsala, and Cox (1999) found, first, that reading motivation predicted the amount of reading, and then that the amount of reading directly predicted reading comprehension performance. Another study by Morgan and Fuchs (2007) found that there was a significant correlation between reading skills and motivation, supporting the possibility of a bidirectional relationship. Based on their results, Morgan and Fuchs argued that researchers, practitioners, and parents might need to target both reading skill and motivation to best help poor readers become proficient in reading.

Influenced by the L1 reading motivation research, reading motivation research for second language (L2) began recently (Grabe, 2009; Grabe & Stroller, 2002). One of the researchers who investigated L2 readers' motivation was Mori (2002, 2004), who explored learners' motivation for reading in English, using an L2 reading motivation questionnaire which was based on Wigfield and Guthrie's Motivation for Reading Questionnaire (MRQ). In one of her studies, she identified four factors influencing the learners' motivation for reading in their second language: the intrinsic value of reading, the importance of reading, extrinsic motivation, and self-efficacy. Consequently, she postulated that expectancy-value theory might possibly be useful in explaining L2 readers' motivation.

Another important study was conducted by Takase (2007), who examined Japanese female high school students' motivation to read extensively both in L1 and L2. She found that two factors, L1 intrinsic motivation and L2 intrinsic motivation, significantly predicted the amount of extensive reading completed by the participants. However, she found that L1 intrinsic motivation was not a significant predictor of L2 intrinsic motivation. More recently, Komiyama (2009) conducted a study with American college L2 learners studying English for academic purposes (EAP). She found that those learners were influenced by both intrinsic and extrinsic motivations for reading. Although these studies have contributed to our understanding of L2 readers' motivation, further research needs to be conducted and much remains to be discovered.

Statement of the Problem

As indicated above, researchers investigating L1 reading have identified the vital role motivation plays in reading performance and achievement. Based on this research, for example, Concept Oriented Reading Instruction (CORI), a type of integrated reading instruction that incorporates both cognitive and affective aspects of reading into reading pedagogy, has been successfully implemented in many primary and secondary schools in the United States (Guthrie, 2008; Guthrie, Wigfield, & Vonsecker, 2000; Swan, 2003; Wigfield & Guthrie, 2010).

L1 reading and L2 reading are inherently similar and they share a number of common aspects because reading, whether in a first or second language involves the reader, the text, and the interaction between the reader and text. This is true regardless of the linguistic, developmental, and sociocultural differences between L1 and L2 reading (Rumelhart, 1977; Singhal, 1998). Therefore, it is reasonable to assume that L2 reading motivation plays as vital a role in L2 learners' reading processes. Yet, in second language contexts, relatively little research has been conducted on the motivation of L2 readers (See Komiyama, 2009; Mori, 2002; and

Takase, 2007 for the few studies concerning L2 reading motivation). As Grabe and Stroller (2002, 2009) have consistently pointed out, further studies are needed to elucidate the exact nature of L2 reading motivation. Specifically, the following aspects of L2 reading motivation have yet to be fully addressed.

The specific components of L2 reading motivation require further identification and clarification. As stated above, several researchers (e.g., Mori, 2002) have explored some components of L2 reading motivation; however, their findings are still at the preliminary stage and need to be validated. For example, a recent study by Cho and Teo (2014) used Mori's reading motivation questionnaire, but could identify only four out of the nine components she originally identified (Mori, 2002). As a result, the researchers have questioned its psychometric properties.

Furthermore, the participants in previous studies (e.g., Mori, 2002; Takase, 2007) were limited to female students or relatively small groups of learners. To allow for wider generalization, larger scale studies that include both male and female participants need to be conducted.

Also, the relationship between L1 reading motivation and L2 reading motivation requires special attention because it may potentially reveal fundamental differences between these two motivations. Takase (2007), for example, has shown that L1 and L2 intrinsic reading motivations are negatively related; however, because of the small number of female high school student participants in her study, this relationship should be re-investigated with a larger sample that includes both male and females.

Purposes and Significance of the Study

The study described in this book aimed at examining the components of L2 learners' reading motivation. This purpose was based on the assumption that L2 reading motivation is domain specific. That is, motivation in the domain of L2 reading is construed as a distinct entity, which is different from other types of motivation in other academic subjects such as history, physics, or mathematics. As the theoretical background of the study, the following three motivation theories in educational psychology were applied: expectancy-value theory, self-determination theory and self-confidence theory.

The second purpose of the study was to investigate the relationships between the components of motivation and L2 reading motivation. It was expected that exploring these relationships would reveal what kind of motivation is influential for L2 reading. In L1 reading, intrinsic motivation is significantly related to successful reading performance. This study might reveal whether the same is true for L2 readers.

The third purpose was to examine the relationship between L1 and L2 intrinsic motivations for reading. It was hoped to discover, for example, whether or not those who love reading in their native language love reading in their L2 language as well. Takase's (2007) results had suggested that L1 and L2 intrinsic motivations for reading were not positively related, especially in the case of less proficient L2 learners whose linguistic resources were limited. It was believed that if the study discussed in this book reached the same conclusions, it consequently might support the linguistic threshold hypothesis (Cummins, 1979) from a motivational perspective. That is that L1 and L2 intrinsic motivations are unrelated unless the L2 learners have reached a linguistic threshold where they can transfer their L1 reading skills to L2 reading tasks (Jiang, 2011).

The study described in this book is significant to the domain of L2 instruction and research for several reasons. First, it extends the knowledge base in L2 reading by identifying the influence of L2 reading motivation on L2 reading behavior. Second, the results of the study contribute to designing research-based reading instruction aimed at enhancing L2 reading motivation and performance. Finally, it may provide individual educators with practical suggestions on how to improve L2 reading instruction in their individual teaching contexts, focusing on affective aspects of learning.

Theoretical Perspectives

The study is guided by four theoretical perspectives: expectancy-value theory, self-determination theory, instrumental orientation, and self-confidence theory. The first two theories have been applied to L1 reading motivation research (Wigfield & Guthrie, 1995, 1997), and the latter two were drawn from previous motivation research in L2 learning.

Expectancy-value theory (Eccles, Wigfield, & Schiefele, 1998) postulates that people's expectancy and value are chief determinants of their behavior and performance. The former concerns the degree to which people believe they can achieve a task. The latter concerns the degree to which they believe that the task is worth pursuing. This theory argues that these two constructs are key components of people's achievement behavior and academic outcomes.

Self-determination theory (Ryan & Deci, 2000) is a motivational theory that is grounded in the belief that people achieve most when they feel they are in charge of their own behavior without external influence or interference from their peers or society. Central to the theory is the distinction between internal and external motivation, depending on where the locus of causality is situated. If people perform a task following their own will, values, and goals, their motivation for the behavior is considered intrinsic because the driving force for the action comes from their own selves. Three essential factors for enhancing intrinsic motivation are competence, autonomy, and relatedness. On the other hand, if people perform a task following outside pressure or coercion, their motivation for the behavior is called extrinsic because the driving force for the action comes from outside their own selves. According to Self-determination theory, extrinsic motivation can be described in four stages, depending on the degree of self-control that individuals have over their actions: external regulation, identification, introjected regulation and integrated regulation.

In addition to these theories from the general motivation literature, concepts of Instrumental orientation (Gardner, 1985) and Self-confidence (Clément, Gardner & Smythe, 1977) were drawn from the second language motivational studies. The former concerns practical benefits of language learning, such as getting a job, and the latter concerns how confident learners feel about their L2 ability.

The Organization of the Book

The organization of the current book is as follows. Chapter 2 reviews the literature on theories of motivation and L1 reading motivation research. Chapter 3 presents an overview of previous L2 reading motivation research. In Chapter 4, methods of the current study are described, including the participants, the instruments used in the studies, the procedures, and the analyses. In Chapter 4, the participants, procedures, instruments, and analyses of the current study are described. In Chapter 5, the results of the reading motivation questionnaire are reported and discussed. In Chapter 6, the L2 reading motivation model is presented and its implications are discussed. In Chapter 7, pedagogical implications are described. Finally, in the final chapter, a brief summary of the study is given, followed by limitations of the study and future research suggestions.

CHAPTER 2
REVIEW OF THE LITERATURE

This chapter reviews part of the literature which the current study draws on. First, 'motivation' is briefly defined, and then the theoretical background and findings of L1 reading motivation research are explained.

Motivation Defined

The word 'motivation' which is derived from the Latin verb *movere* (to move), "signifies a condition that gets us going, keeps us working, and helps us complete tasks" (Schunk, Pintrich, & Meece, 2008, p. 4). Motivation accounts for *antecedents* (i.e., causes and origins) of action, that is, why people do something, how much effort they exert, and how long they persist in engaging in the action (Dörnyei, 2001). In the first half of the twentieth century, dominant views, such as those represented in Freud's work, connected motivation with inner forces, including instincts, traits, and volition. By the mid-twentieth century, behaviorists regarded motivation as "a change in the rate, frequency of occurrence, or form of behavior (response) as a function of environmental events and stimuli" (Schunk, Pintrich, & Meece, 2008, p. 20). 1960's humanistic psychologists, such as Carl Rogers and Abraham Maslow, proposed that the central motivating force is the self-actualizing tendency, which involves people's desire to pursue personal growth and develop their capacities and talents fully. More recently, motivation researchers have focused on individual mental processes or cognitions as the chief driving force of human actions and behavior. That is, such mental processes as ideas, thoughts, beliefs, goals, and self-representation of events influence human actions and behavior (Eccles & Wigfield, 2002; Jarvis, 2005).

Based on this cognitive perspective, motivation can be defined as "the process whereby goal-directed activity is instigated and sustained "(Schunk, Pintrich, & Meece, 2008, p. 4). This definition presupposes the following: (a) motivation is a process rather than a product; (b) motivation involves goals that provide impetus for action; (c) motivation requires activity that includes effort, persistence, and volition; and (d) motivated activity is triggered and maintained by expectations, attributions, and affects.

Although a number of competing or alternative theories of motivation have emerged to date, cognitive psychologists share several basic assumptions about motivation (Schunk, Pintrich, & Meece, 2008). As mentioned above, one assumption is that motivation encompasses individual cognitions, such as beliefs, thoughts, goals, and the mental processes that guide achievement-related actions. Another assumption is that motivation is a complex phenomenon that consists of a host of social, contextual, and personal variables including self-regulation, self-efficacy, interest, goal-setting, and attributions of success and failure. So 'motivation' is not a unitary construct; rather, it is a composite of multiple constructs that interact and change under the influence of different contextual and individual factors. Another assumption is that motivation is not static; it changes with human development. Therefore, learners' developmental stages have to be taken into account in any study of motivation. A final shared assumption concerns individual differences in motivational processes. It is assumed that individual characteristics, such as cultural background, socioeconomic status, ethnicity, gender, and ability level exert significant influences on motivational processes;

consequently, it is necessary to take individual differences into consideration in explaining motivational processes.

In sum, the current views of motivation recognize individual cognitions as a key factor in people's behavior (Pintrich, 2003; Pintrich & Schunk, 1996). Researchers claim that motivation determines why individuals choose or do not choose to engage in different activities, the degree of persistence, and the amount of effort they expend in doing the activities (Eccles, Wigfield, & Shiefele, 1998; Wigfield, 2000). In line with this cognitive perspective, several motivation theories, such as achievement motivation theory, self-efficacy theory, attribution theory, goal setting theory, self-determination theory and social motivation theory, have emerged.

Theories of Motivation Applied to the L1 Reading Domain

Research into first language reading provides a logical comparison and basis for research into second language reading. In the following section three motivation theories that have been applied to the domain of L1 reading are discussed: expectancy-value theory, self-efficacy theory, and self-determination theory.

Expectancy-Value Theory

Expectancy-value theory is one of the most widely acknowledged sub-theories of achievement theory, which defines achievement motivation as the desire to show competence in activities (Eccles, Wigfield, & Schiefele, 1998; Elliot & Church, 1997; Pintrich & Schunk, 1996). This theory addresses two important questions about behavior: "Can I do this task successfully?" and "Why do I want to perform this task?" In other words, the theory proposes that achievement is the result both of individuals' expectation of performing successfully and of the value that is attached to the potentially successful outcome (Eccles 1983; Wigfield, 1994; Wigfield & Eccles, 1992, 2000, 2002; Wigfield, Eccles, & Rodriguez, 1998; Wigfield, Tonks, & Eccles, 2004).

The expectancy component of this theory consists of two variables: individuals' belief in their own ability and their 'expectancy' of success. The former involves individuals' evaluations of their competence in different areas and predicts their performance in different domains, such as reading and mathematics (Eccles, Wigfield, Harold, & Blumenfeld, 1993). For example, if individuals feel they are competent players, they are more likely to perform well in their sport. The latter variable, individuals' beliefs about how well they will do on upcoming tasks either in the immediate or distant future, also affects their performance (Eccles & Wigfield, 2002). If they have high expectations for success, they are likely to persist in performing the task and show better outcomes (Wigfield, Byrnes, Eccles, 2006, Wigfield & Eccles, 1992). On the other hand, if they have low expectancies for success, most individuals will not engage in the task because they expect that they will perform poorly or fail. Furthermore, even if they are interested in the task, if they experience failure repeatedly, they will eventually choose not to engage in the task (Schunk, Pintrich, & Meece, 2008). For instance, even if a person is fond of singing, she may stop singing entirely after continuously receiving negative reactions to her singing from her peers.

The value component of this theory addresses the question of what value people find in engaging in particular activities. That is, even if people believe that they are capable of being successful in an activity, they might not engage in it unless they identify value or meaning in performing it.

This component can be classified into four categories: attainment value or importance, intrinsic value, utility value or usefulness, and cost (Wigfield, 1997; Zimmerman & Schunk, 2008). Attainment value can be defined as the perceived importance of doing well on a given task, such as math or sports. This is closely linked to individuals' identity. Intrinsic value or interest reflects how much individuals are interested in or like the activity in itself. Utility value, or the usefulness of the activity, concerns individuals' inherent sense of its relevance to meeting needs or wants and to plans for their future. For example, an activity might have utility value if it satisfied course requirements or enabled the achievement of a good job even if it was uninteresting. The last category, cost, is related to the perceived effort of accomplishing an activity, such as the time needed and sacrifices to be made. In sum, proponents of expectancy-value theory argue that individuals' beliefs about their abilities and value influence their achievement motivation.

Self-Efficacy Theory

A construct similar to the expectancy component of Expectancy-Value Theory is Self-efficacy theory (Bandura, 1997,; Pajares, 1996, Schunk, 1991). Self-efficacy can be defined as "people's judgment of their capabilities to organize and execute courses of action required to attain designated types of performances" (Bandura, 1986, p. 391). Bandura has contended that individuals' self-efficacy belief or expectation about how well they can accomplish a given task, is one of the major factors that determine activity choice, willingness to expend effort, and perseverance. If individuals perceive that they can carry out an upcoming task successfully, they are willing to expend effort to accomplish the task. Conversely, when they expect that they cannot perform the task well, they are unlikely to make an effort to accomplish it. Bandura (2004) has proposed that self-efficacy beliefs provide the foundation for human motivation, well-being, and personal accomplishment. He has also contended that efficacy-beliefs are domain-specific and task-specific. That is, learners possess different degrees and types of ability beliefs, depending on the nature of the specific task they are engaged in. In other words, beliefs in one's ability are more closely related to particular task performance than to general efficacy beliefs.

According to Bandura (1997), there are four sources that students use to shape their self-efficacy beliefs. The most prominent source is *experience* of *mastery*, the interpreted results of one's own achievements. In school, students are constantly evaluated on their performance in academic subjects, receiving grades or feedback from teachers and peers. Through these evaluations, students form their interpretations of their own abilities, which then become one of the major sources of their competence beliefs. If students constantly receive high grades or evaluations, they develop a high sense of self-efficacy whereas if they continually receive low evaluations, they are likely to feel less confident about their abilities in school work.

The second source of self-efficacy beliefs is students' interpretations of the *vicarious experiences* of others. Observing other students with similar abilities perform tasks, students build expectations on whether or not they can perform similar tasks. For example, if students see a classmate succeed in giving a presentation in a second language they both study, it is likely that they will think they can do it, too. On the other hand, if they see a classmate fail in the task, it is more likely that they will think they cannot succeed in it either. Vicarious experience also involves comparisons with others because in school contexts, students are put in situations where they are constantly compared with others. Through these comparisons, students form interpretations of their own achievements, which then influence their self-efficacy beliefs.

Verbal messages and social persuasions from societal influences like the media and from people who surround students like parents, relatives, teachers, and peers also create self-efficacy beliefs. Students grow up listening to various messages about what they should accomplish in their academic work. These messages inform students' judgments of their own abilities, which eventually form their self-efficacy beliefs.

Students' self-beliefs are also influenced by their physiological and emotional states; for example, anxiety, stress, mood, and state of health all affect the way they see themselves. If students are in a positive and optimistic mood, they are likely to have enhanced self-efficacy, whereas if they are depressed or stressed, they are likely to have diminished self-efficacy. This suggests self-efficacy beliefs are not constant because such beliefs are likely to be influenced by individuals' mental and physical conditions. To conclude, these four internal and external sources shape students' perceptions of their academic achievement, and, in turn, these perceptions inform self-efficacy beliefs, which then influence academic motivation and eventual success or lack of it. Research on self-efficacy has suggested that learners' academic self-efficacy not only influences their academic performance but also mediates the effect of such knowledge, skills, and other motivational factors (Pajares, 1996). It follows that when educators foster students' positive self-efficacy beliefs, it can encourage learners to tackle challenging tasks with more perseverance and effort.

Self-Determination Theory

Another major theory applied to L1 reading motivation research is self-determination theory (SDT). This theory addresses social-contextual conditions that promote the natural processes of self-motivation and healthy psychological development (Deci & Ryan, 1985a, 1985b; Ryan & Deci, 2000). The central tenet of this theory is the distinction between two types of behaviors, one that emanates from one's sense of self and the other that stems from outside of one's self (Deci, Vallerland, Pelletier, & Ryan, 1991; Kowal & Fortier, 1999; Ryan & Deci, 2000).

This distinction can be explained by the concept of "the locus of causality" (Ryan & Deci, 2000). When a behavior is determined by one's self, the locus of causality is internal to one's self; therefore, the regulatory process involves making a "choice" for oneself. Such behaviors are performed out of interest and curiosity, thereby satisfying one's innate psychological needs for competence and autonomy. However, when a behavior is controlled by outside factors, the locus of causality is external to the self; therefore, the regulatory process involves "compliance"(Deci, Vallerland, Pelletier, & Ryan, 1991, p. 327). Such behaviors are performed due to outside pressure or control.

Intrinsic motivation is defined as "the doing of an activity for its inherent satisfactions rather than for some separable consequence" (Ryan & Deci, 2000, p. 56). An intrinsically motivated person is spontaneously moved to act for the fun or challenge that accompanies the given task rather than because of external pressures, punishments, or rewards. For example, when people become absorbed in reading a mystery story just for the fun of it, they are intrinsically motivated to read because they engage in the act of reading based on their inner desire to do and the personal reward they experience from the activity. Another example is that when people play a musical instrument because of the sense of satisfaction and enjoyment they experience, they are intrinsically motivated.

The focus on intrinsic motivation within self-determination theory is explained by a sub-theory known as cognitive evaluation theory

(CET) (Deci & Ryan, 1985a; Ryan & Deci, 2000). CET suggests that social environments can facilitate or destroy intrinsic motivation by supporting or blocking people's fulfilment of their psychological needs. CET is based on the findings of empirical research and is primarily focused on three psychological needs, "competence, autonomy, and relatedness, which, when satisfied, yield enhanced self-motivation and mental health and, when prevented, lead to decreased motivation and self-being" (Ryan & Deci, 2000, p. 68). Deci, Vallerland, Pelletier, and Ryan (1991) defined 'competence' as "one's perceived abilities in performing given tasks" and "being efficacious in performing the requisite actions". They defined 'relatedness' as "developing secure and satisfying connections with others in one's social environment"; and 'autonomy' as "being self-initiating and self-regulating of one's own actions" (p. 327). CET posits that these three factors are essential for positive, energized behaviors and the enhancement of intrinsic motivation because, in the absence of any one of them, it is difficult to foster positive motivation, and it is this form of motivation that is believed to result in high-quality learning and creativity (Ryan & Deci, 2000).

Extrinsic motivation, on the other hand, refers to behaviors that are considered a means to an end (Deci & Ryan, 1985a, 1985b; Deci, Vallerand, Pelletier, & Ryan, 1991). Hence, extrinsically motivated behaviors are instrumental in nature because they are performed not out of a deep-seated interest in the activity, but to attain some other outcomes. For instance, if students do their homework to avoid being scolded by their teachers, their actions are extrinsically motivated because they have engaged in the activity to avoid punishment. Or if students study English to pass an entrance examination or attain a qualification, they are extrinsically motivated because their action is driven by the desire to attain the external outcome of passing the test, not by any intrinsic interest in the test itself.

Deci and Ryan (1985a) identified four types of extrinsically motivated behaviors, and proposed a second sub-theory, the organismic integration theory (OIT), which is subdivided into four different types of motivation, according to the degree of self-determination involved. These four types of extrinsic motivation are external regulation, introjection, identification, and integrated regulation. Figure 1 illustrates the OIT taxonomy of motivation, arranged by degree to which behavior emanates from the self.

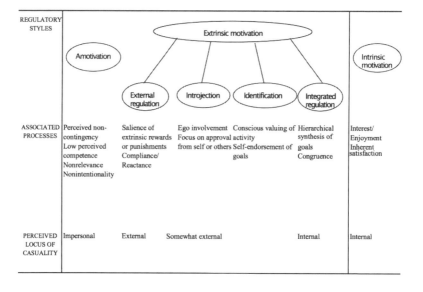

Figure 1. The Types of Motivation in Self-Determination Theory (Deci & Ryan, 2000).

At the far left of the self-determination continuum is amotivation, or the state of lacking an intention to act. This state is caused by not valuing an activity, not feeling capable of doing it, or not believing that it will lead to a desired outcome (Ryan & Deci, 2000). At the far right is intrinsic motivation, the state of doing an activity for its own enjoyment or interest. Extrinsically motivated behaviors cover the continuum between these two types of motivation, varying in the degree of self-determination.

The least self-determined behaviors are referred to as motivated by external regulation. Such behaviors are performed to satisfy external demands or to receive rewards, not out of interest in the activity. The locus of control is outside of the person. Thus, if children stop playing a video game because they are afraid of being punished by their parents, they are externally regulated.

'Introjected regulation' is a type of extrinsic motivation, which involves following a regulation but not fully accepting it as one's own decision. If students submit homework on time because they do not want to be regarded as lazy, or because they want to appear to be competent, their action reflects introjected regulation, or "internal coercion" (Deci, Vallerand, Pelletier, & Ryan, 1991, p. 329). The locus of control is somewhat external, and behaviors are performed to avoid guilt or anxiety or to demonstrate ability and boost self-worth.

A more autonomous type of motivation is 'identified regulation'. This occurs when individuals have come to consciously value the behavior themselves, and have accepted it as personally important (Ryan & Deci, 2000). If students choose to do extra work outside of the classroom because they believe it will help them improve their performance at school, this behavior shows identified regulation. This behavior is still externally regulated because it is performed primarily because of its usefulness in achieving the goal of improving school grades, and not because of interest or enjoyment.

The least controlled and most autonomous form of motivation is 'integrated regulation'. Integrated regulation occurs when "identified regulations have been fully assimilated by the self" (Ryan & Deci, 2000, p. 62). That is, people integrate the value of the behavior into "their own self-schemas and engage in behavior because of its importance to their senses of self" (Schunk, Pintrich, & Meece, 2008, p. 243). For example, when people often exercise because they believe that it will lead to better health, this reflects integrated regulation. That is, they exercise not because it is inherently fun, but because they strongly believe that exercise will help them live the comfortable and healthy life which they value. Although integrated regulation shares many qualities with intrinsic motivation, there is one distinct difference. The former is carried out to achieve a valued outcome beyond performing the action itself, but the latter is done for the inherent satisfaction gained from performing the action.

As discussed above, self-determination theory makes a critical distinction between intrinsic and extrinsic motivations, that is, volitional behaviors that emanate from one's sense of self and those performed because of outside pressure or control. This theory postulates that promoting greater self-determination, that is, more self-initiated behaviors, is an important developmental goal. Further, it claims that support for learners' feeling of competence, autonomy, and relatedness is essential for human development (Ryan & Deci, 2000).

These three motivational theories described above have been applied to L1 reading motivation research as the theoretical framework. Table 1 summarizes the characteristics of the theories, including basic assumptions, theory components and major studies.

Table 1. *Characteristics of Theories of Motivation Applied to L1 Reading Motivation*

Theory	Basic assumption	Components	Major studies
Expectancy-value	Motivation is the desire to show competence in activities.	· Value · Expectancy	Eccles, Wigfield, & Schiefele, 1998
Self-efficacy	Individuals' competence beliefs control what and how they perform.	· Performance outcomes · Vicarious experiences · Verbal persuasion · Physiological feedback	Bandura, 1986, 1995, 1997, 2001
Self-determination	Motivation is influenced by the degrees of self-control over the choices individuals make.	· Intrinsic motivation · Integrated regulation · Identification · Introjection · External regulation · Amotivation	Deci & Ryan, 1985a Ryan & Deci, 2000

Because these theories are concerned with human motivation, they naturally share some common features. For instance, the expectancy component of expectancy-value theory resembles self-efficacy beliefs because both of them are concerned with individuals' perceptions of their own abilities to perform a certain task (Wigfield & Eccles, 2000). Similarly, self-determination theory (SDT) and the value component of expectancy-value theory (EVT) share some common features (Wigfield & Eccles, 2000). To be specific, the similarities between SDT and EVT can be found among the following components. First, intrinsic motivation (SDT) and intrinsic value (EVT) are similar because both of them address internal regulation for doing something because one is inherently interested in doing it for its own sake. (Eccles & Wigfield, 2002). Second, integrated regulation (SDT) and attainment value (EVT) are similar because both of them represent the personal value attached to a particular activity because it is instrumental in achieving a desired goal. Third, identified regulation (SDT) and utility value (EVT) are closely related in that both of them are concerned with the internalized value attached to a task because achieving the task will contribute to one's successful career or life.

In summary, L1 reading motivation research draws on the three theories described above, and they share some common aspects. This is one of the reasons why reading motivation research into L1 reading refers to multiple theories rather than a single one in order to explain motivation for reading (Wigfield & Eccles, 2000).

Research on Motivation for L1 Reading

Research on the role of motivation in reading began in the United States in the early 1990s. Since then, numerous studies have been conducted, focusing on the components of reading motivation and their relationship to reading achievement. The findings of these studies have consistently demonstrated the multifaceted nature of reading motivation and its central role in literacy development (e.g., Cole, 2002; Guthrie & Alao, 1997; Guthrie, Wigfield, & Perencevich, 2004; Wang & Guthrie, 2004). The background of the reading motivation research is described, including the definition of L1 reading motivation, the components of L1 reading motivation, and the probable relationship between L1 reading motivation and performance.

The Background of the Research on L1 Reading Motivation

There are three major reasons why research on reading motivation began in the early 1990s, according to Wigfield (1997). The first reason concerns the fact that until then, reading research had mainly been focused on cognitive aspects of reading, leaving affective aspects of L1 reading unexplored (Guthrie & Wigfield, 1997). Wigfield (1997) argued that it was necessary to take affective aspects into consideration because by nature reading was an effortful and conscious activity that could be easily influenced by individual attitudes and emotions.

The second reason concerns the need to explain reading behavior in light of new motivational theories such as expectancy-value theory or self-determination theory described in the previous chapter. Researchers believed that these theories would be instrumental in explicating L1 reader's reading processes. The third reason concerns the domain specific nature of motivation. Until then, research on motivation had been focused on motivation as a whole, and researchers had not considered how motivation might differ in different domains (Wigfield, 1997). It was pointed out, however, that there was a specific need to explore the domain specific nature of motivation, for example, in reading, science, sports, language, and music (Bandura, 1997; Schunk & Zimmerman, 2006).

Reading Motivation Defined

Reading motivation has been defined as "the individual's personal goals, values, and beliefs with regard to the topics, processes, and aspects of reading" (Guthrie & Wigfield, 2000, p. 405). This definition is grounded in the 'engagement perspective' described by Guthrie & Wigfield, (2000) which integrates cognitive, motivational, and social aspects of reading. This perspective can be explained by four principles: (a) engagement in reading refers to motivated and strategic interaction with text; (b) engaged reading promotes reading comprehension; (c) engaged reading and its components (motivation and cognitive strategies) can be deliberately increased by instructional practices; and (d) an instructional framework that merges motivational and cognitive strategy support in reading can enhance engaged reading and reading comprehension (Baker, Afferback, & Reinking, 1996; Guthrie & Alvermann, 1999). Furthermore, the engagement perspective assumes that engaged readers are motivated, strategic, knowledgeable, and socially interactive, and that they "read for different purposes, utilize knowledge gained from previous experience to generate new understandings, and participate in meaningful social interactions around reading" (Baker & Wigfield, 1999).

Components of L1 Reading Motivation

In conceptualizing reading motivation, Wigfield and Guthrie (1997) assumed that there were a variety of motives for reading that could influence reading achievement. They based this view of reading motivation on self-efficacy theory, self-determination theory, and expectancy-value theory. Drawing on these theories as well as on a previous study by Guthrie, Van Meter, et al., (1996), Wigfield and Guthrie (1997) hypothesized that L1 reading motivation is composed of three components and 11 sub-components (Table 2).

Table 2. *Proposed Aspects of Reading Motivation (Wigfield, 1997)*

Competence and reading efficacy	Achievement values and goals	Social aspects of reading
Reading efficacy Reading challenge Reading work Avoidance	**Intrinsic motivation** Reading curiosity Reading involvement Importance of L2 Reading **Extrinsic motivation** Competition in reading Reading recognition Reading for grades	Social reasons for reading Reading compliance

The first component is related to individuals' beliefs about their competency or ability. The sub-components are reading efficacy, reading challenge, and work avoidance. The second component is related to theories of intrinsic-extrinsic motivation, values, and goals. The sub-components are intrinsic motivation (reading curiosity, reading involvement, importance of L2 reading) and extrinsic motivation (competition in reading, reading for recognition, and reading for grades). The last component is related to social aspects of reading, and the subcomponents are social reasons for reading and reading compliance.

The Development of the Motivation for Reading Questionnaire

In order to measure motivation for L1 reading, Wigfield and Guthrie (1995, 1997) developed the Motivation for Reading Questionnaire (MRQ). This questionnaire was administered to 100 elementary school pupils in the United States. Statistical analyses were conducted to assess the proposed dimensions of reading motivation and to determine whether the items had good psychometric qualities. The results showed that many of the proposed aspects were measured with adequate internal consistency and reliability. The most clearly identified aspects according to Wigfield, (1997) were social reasons for reading, reading competition, reading work avoidance, reading efficacy, reading recognition, reading curiosity, and reading involvement (see Table 3 for sample items).

Table 3. *Sample Items from the Motivation for Reading Questionnaire (Wigfield, 1997)*

Construct	Example item
Reading Efficacy	I am a good reader.
Reading Challenge	I like hard, challenging books.
Reading Curiosity	I like to read about new things.
Reading Involvement	I read stories about fantasy and make-believe.
Importance of L1 Reading	It is very important to me to be a good reader.
Competition in Reading	I try to get more answers right than my friends.
Reading Recognition	I like having the teacher say I read well.
Reading for Grades	I read to improve my grades.
Social Reasons for Reading	I talk to my friends about what I am reading.
Reading Compliance	I always do my reading exactly as the teacher wants it.
Reading Work Avoidance	I don't like reading something when the words are too difficult.

In the second stage of the study, a final 54-item Motivation for Reading Questionnaire (MRQ) was created. This revised questionnaire was administered to 600 children (Wigfield, Wilde, Baker, Fernandez-Fein, & Scher, 1996). Confirmatory factor analyses were conducted to validate the questionnaire. The results supported the multidimensionality of reading motivation with adequate internal consistency and reliability (Wigfield, 1997).

The Relationship Between Reading Motivation and Reading Performance

The MRQ was used in a number of studies designed to explore the relationship between reading motivation and reading performance (e.g., Baker & Wigfield, 1999; Guthrie, Hoa, Wigfield, Tonks, & Perencevich, 2006; Guthrie, Wigfield, Metsala, & Cox 1999; Wang & Guthrie, 2004). Many of these studies demonstrated the close connection between reading motivation and reading performance.

Children's Reading Motivation, Reading Amount and Text Comprehension

Wigfield and Guthrie (1997) explored aspects of reading motivation and how these aspects related to the amount and breadth of reading. The participants were 105 pupils at an elementary school who completed the MRQ twice during the school year. The amount and breadth of their reading were measured by two inventories, the Reading Activity Inventory (RAI) (Guthrie, McGough, & Wigfield, 1994) and the keeping of reading logs. The former consisted of questions such as how often and what kind of books the children read in and out of school. The latter was a reading log in which students kept a record of reading hours outside school. The results confirmed that their motivation for reading predicted the amount and breadth of their reading and also confirmed the multi-dimensional nature of children's motivation to read. Moreover, an intrinsic component predicted the amount of reading more strongly than an extrinsic component.

Guthrie et al. (1999) explored how motivational variables contributed to reading achievement and text comprehension in two studies (Study 1 and Study 2). Study 1 was conducted with 271 grade school students (117 fifth-graders and 154 third-graders). The data were drawn from a performance assessment administered at the end of the school year. The assessment included two measures of text comprehension, prior knowledge relevant to the comprehension measures, the MRQ, reading efficacy, and amount of reading. The results revealed that the amount of reading significantly predicted text comprehension even when the contributions of past reading achievement, prior topic knowledge, self-efficacy for reading, and reading motivation were statistically controlled.

Study 2 was conducted to investigate the generalizability of the results of Study 1 to older students. The sample (17,424 eighth- and tenth-graders) for this study was drawn from the National Educational Longitudinal Study (NELS) database. The measures used in the NELS database included a comprehension test, a reading amount question, two reading motivation questions, and two reading efficacy questions. As was true in Study 1, the results revealed that the amount of reading significantly predicted text comprehension after controlling for other variables. They also showed that reading motivation predicated the amount of reading. These findings pointed to a close connection between reading motivation, amount of reading, and text comprehension.

In another study of elementary students, Baker and Wigfield (1999) investigated dimensions of children's motivation for reading and the relationships of these to reading activity and reading achievement. The first goal of the study was to assess the proposed dimensions of the MRQ with a larger number of participants, using confirmatory factor analysis. The second goal was to further examine links between reading motivation, achievement, and amount of reading by replicating Wigfield and Guthrie's

(1997) study. A final goal was to examine whether different dimensions of reading motivation varied with factors such as the students' gender, grade, and ethnicity. The participants in the study were 371 children in six elementary schools in the United States. The measures included the MRQ and several other measures of reading activity and reading achievement. Confirmatory factor analysis results indicated that the proposed dimensions of students' reading motivation did exist and were measured reliably. Based on the results of the confirmatory factor analysis, scale scores for each of the reading motivation dimensions were created. All these scores correlated positively with one another except for the score for the desire to avoid reading. Mean scale scores differed by gender and ethnicity, with girls and African Americans reporting higher motivation; most of the scales were positively related to students' report of reading activities and achievement. Cluster analyses identified seven groups of students based on their motivational profiles related to reading activity and reading achievement. As in previous studies (Wigfield & Guthrie, 1997, 1999), this study demonstrated that reading motivation has several different dimensions and that these dimensions have a close relationship with reading performance.

More recently, Wang and Guthrie (2004) investigated the relationship between text comprehension and the effects of intrinsic and extrinsic motivation, amount of reading, and past reading achievement in the United States and China, respectively. In their research six motivational constructs, which had been initially proposed by Wigfield and Guthrie (1997, 1999), were hypothesized to influence reading motivation: reading efficacy, curiosity, involvement, recognition, grades, and compliance. A theoretical structural model of text comprehension that was intended to describe "the direct and indirect relationships among intrinsic motivation, extrinsic motivation, amount of reading for school, amount of reading for personal enjoyment, past reading achievement, and text comprehension" (p. 166) was developed and tested using structural equation modelling. The participants in the study consisted of 187 American and 197 Chinese fourth-grade elementary school pupils. The measures used by the study were the Motivation for Reading Questionnaire, the Reading Activity Inventory, the Evaluation of Educational Achievement Reading Literacy Test, and reading grades based on teacher evaluations during the previous semester. The structural equation modelling results supported the hypothesis that intrinsic and extrinsic motivations have different relationships with text comprehension. Intrinsic motivation was positively associated with text comprehension in both of the groups when the other variables were controlled. Extrinsic motivation, however, was negatively related to text comprehension in both of the groups after controlling for other variables. In both groups the amount of reading was not significantly related to text comprehension. Based on these findings, Wang and Guthrie pointed to the importance of intrinsic motivation in text comprehension, in particular, curiosity for reading. They concluded "intrinsic motivation is pivotal to successful reading in American and Chinese children" (p. 182).

Summary of L1 Reading Motivation Research

This chapter presented an overview of research on the part motivation plays in L1 reading, focusing on how that research had developed over the last three decades. One of the major reasons why reading motivation research began in the United States was the growing concern over children's declining interest in reading across the country. Educators felt that it was necessary to have children read more and, as a result, saw a need to address their motivation for reading.

Cognitive views of motivation were presented, and reading motivation was defined as individuals' personal goals, values, and beliefs concerning what and how they read. To describe motivated readers, measures of engagement were introduced. The conclusion of many studies was that, in order to get students engaged in reading, it is necessary for educators to integrate cognitive, motivational, and social aspects of reading in their lessons and that if instructional practices promote the integration of these three aspects, reading engagement is deepened.

CHAPTER 3
L2 READING MOTIVATION RESEARCH

Chapter 3 first introduces some of the major studies conducted into L2 reading motivation and then the areas requiring further investigation are noted.

Research on Motivation for L2 Reading

During the last decade, several empirical studies have investigated the components of L2 reading motivation and their influences on L2 learners' reading performance and behavior. Table 4 outlines some of the major studies and includes the theoretical framework, participants, and components of motivation identified in them.

Table 4. *L2 Reading Motivation Studies*

Researcher	Theoretical framework	Participants	Components of L2 reading Motivation
Mori (2002)	Expectancy Value Theory Integrative Orientation	447 female Japanese female college students	Reading Efficacy Intrinsic Value of Reading Extrinsic Utility Value of Reading Importance of L2 Reading

35

Nishino (2005)	Same as Mori's (2002a)	262 Japanese high school students	Intrinsic Value of Reading Importance of L2 Reading Reading Efficacy Intrinsic Value of Reading Communicative Orientation
Dhanapala (2006)	Expectancy value theory, Self-determination theory	123 Sri Lankan college students & 124 Japanese college students	Curiosity Involvement Preference for Challenge Recognition Grades Social Reading Competition Compliance
Takase (2007)	Studies on L2 learning (e.g., Gardner, 1985) and educational psychology (Wigfield, 1997)	219 Japanese female high school students	Intrinsic motivation for L1 reading Intrinsic motivation for L2 reading Parents' involvement in and family attitudes toward reading Entrance exam-related extrinsic motivation Fondness for written materials Internet-related instrumental motivation

Komiyama (2009)	Self-determination theory (Deci & Ryan, 1985) and the Motivation for Reading Questionnaire (Wang & Guthrie, 2004)	2,018 students enrolled in 53 English language programs at American colleges and universities	Curiosity Involvement Preference for challenge Recognition Grades Social sharing Competition Compliance

Mori (2002) was the probably the first recognized researcher to explore L2 reading motivation in Japan. The purpose of her study was to identify what factors resulted in motivation to read in English for 447 Japanese female college students in an EFL setting. The instrument she used was a 30-item questionnaire based on the Motivation for Reading Questionnaire which Wigfield & Guthrie (1997) had created for L1 readers. She had modified the questionnaire by adding one L2 specific factor, Integrative Motivation, which was designed to tap into L2 learners' desire to be integrated in the community where the target language (L2) is spoken (Gardner, 1985). After a factor analysis of the questionnaire data, she extracted four factors with adequate reliabilities: Intrinsic Value of Reading, Extrinsic Utility Value of Reading, Importance of L2 Reading, and Reading Efficacy. These factors accounted for 56% of the total variance in reading motivation.

These results indicated some similarities and differences from the results in L1 reading. In an L1 study, Wigfield and Guthrie (1997) had identified seven components of reading motivation: Social Reasons for Reading, Reading Competition, Reading Work Avoidance, Reading Efficacy, Reading Recognition, Reading Curiosity, and Reading Involvement. Of these, Mori identified Reading Efficacy and Importance of Reading while the other four factors (Reading Curiosity, Reading

Involvement, Reading Avoidance, and Reading Challenge) clustered into a factor which she named Intrinsic Value of Reading. Mori speculated that this was due to the fact that intrinsic value underlies these four factors.

Based on these results, Mori indicated that the components of L2 reading motivation appear to resemble those of expectancy value theory (expectancy for success, attainment value, intrinsic value, extrinsic utility value, and cost). Accordingly, she suggested that L2 reading motivation can be explained by a general motivational model based on expectancy-value theory.

Another of her important findings was that Gardner's concept of integrative orientation was not identified as an independent construct of L2 reading motivation. Mori postulated that this was probably due to the fact that the study was conducted in an EFL environment where the learners' desire to be integrated into the target community is not as strong as that of ESL (English as the second language) learners (Warden & Hsui, 2000). In conclusion, Mori suggested that it was necessary to conduct further studies using expectancy-value theory as the theoretical framework of L2 reading motivation.

More recently in Japan, Takase (2007) investigated 219 Japanese female high school students' motivation for extensive reading. The purpose of the study was threefold: to investigate the components of L2 reading motivation of Japanese high school students, to find predictor(s) of their motivation to read English books and to examine the relationship between the students' reading motivation and their performance in Japanese and English.

The instruments consisted of a reading motivation questionnaire, an English test, and the participants' reading records. The 45-item questionnaire was based on studies in the field of L2 learning (e.g., Mori, 2002) and L1 reading motivation research (e.g., Wigfield & Guthrie, 1997).

The English test was the Secondary Language English Proficiency (SLEP) test. The amount which the students read in both their first and second languages was checked, using their book records. The questionnaire was administered after the participants had completed a one-year extensive reading course.

The questionnaire results, test scores, and reading amount were analyzed using a Pearson product-moment correlational analysis, factor analysis, and regression analysis. The correlation analysis showed that the amount of reading and the test scores had a low but significant correlation of $r = .25$; however, the number of books read in Japanese and the amount read in English were not significantly related.

The factor analysis of the questionnaire data yielded six factors: (a) Intrinsic Motivation for L1 Reading, (b) Intrinsic Motivation for L2 Reading, (c) Parents' Involvement in and Family Attitudes toward Reading, (d) Entrance Exam-Related Extrinsic Motivation, (e) Fondness for Written Materials, and (f) Internet-Related Instrumental Motivation and Negative Attitude Toward Extensive Reading. The regression analysis showed that Intrinsic Motivation both in L1 and L2 accounted for more variance in the amount and breadth of reading than extrinsic motivation.

This study is noteworthy in that its results demonstrated some interesting differences from Mori's study (2002). First, an extrinsic motivation factor related to college entrance examinations was identified. Takase explained that this was because her participants were high school students who had to prepare themselves for competitive college entrance examinations in Japan while Mori's participants were college learners who had already taken such examinations. This suggests that test-related extrinsic motivation for reading English is an influential factor for Japanese high school learners. Another difference is that Takase identified a social factor, Parents' Involvement in and Family Attitudes toward Reading. Although this factor might be more influential in L1 reading, this study indicated that social aspects also need to be considered as influences on L2 reading motivation. The third notable finding is that there was no significant correlation between L1 and L2 reading motivations; that is, they should be seen as separate constructs. Takase explained, "Almost no relationship was found between the participants' L1 and L2 reading performance. Interviews with so-called bookworms… revealed that their L1 reading habits did not influence their L2 English reading" (2007, p. 11). In short, avid L1 readers do not necessarily become avid readers in L2. This finding can be explained by the language threshold hypothesis, which posits that "language knowledge is more important than L1 reading abilities up to some point at which the learner has enough L2 knowledge to read reasonably fluently" (Grabe & Stoller, 2002, p. 50). Hence, this result suggests that even if students enjoy reading in their L1, they may not necessarily enjoy reading in L2 unless they have reached a certain level of L2 reading proficiency.

More recently, in the context of English for Academic Purposes (EAP) in the United States, Komiyama (2009) conducted a study on ESL adult learners' motivation to read. Her research questions addressed (a) the multidimensionality of EAP reading motivation; (b) distinct motivational patterns among groups of students, (c) the relationships between motivation and learner variables, and (d) associations between motivation and L2 text comprehension. The participants were 2,018 students (1,037 male and 980 female students) enrolled in 53 English language programs. They came to the United States from 92 different countries where 56 different languages were spoken as the first language. Their ages ranged from 18 to 68, and the average age was 24. Their main purpose for studying English was to prepare themselves for their studies at American colleges and universities.

One of the instruments was an L2 reading motivation questionnaire designed to measure two major factors, intrinsic and extrinsic motivation, proposed by self-determination theory (Wang & Guthrie, 2004). The other one was an L2 text comprehension test. The questionnaire and test were shipped to the 53 institutions where 1,400 students responded to the instruments. The resulting statistical analyses indicated that EAP learners' motivation for reading was composed of intrinsic motivation and three types of extrinsic motivation (extrinsic drive to excel, extrinsic academic compliance, and extrinsic social sharing). Furthermore, the results of a cluster analysis revealed five motivational profiles among the learners. Interestingly, students with low motivational profiles scored higher on the test than those with higher motivational profiles. Komiyama speculated that this was probably due to the influence of their L1 backgrounds on the test performance. In conclusion, she pointed to the role of intrinsic motivation for L2 reading as the vital factor in characterizing L2 motivation for reading.

Summary of L2 Reading Motivation Research

In this section, several major studies on L2 reading motivation were presented. Although the number of studies is still limited, they have produced important findings concerning the nature of L2 reading motivation. To be specific, as has been demonstrated in L1 reading motivation research, L2 reading motivation is not a unitary construct, but multidimensional, consisting of several motivational factors. Although the identified factors still require further validation, L2 reading motivation can be potentially explained by such motivation theories as expectancy-value theory and self-determination theory, which were also applied to L1 reading motivation research. As has been found in Komiyama's study (2012), intrinsic motivation and different types of extrinsic motivation appear to be the main components of L2 reading motivation. In terms of theories of motivation specifically aimed at L2 learners, integrative orientation for L2 reading did not emerge as one of these distinct factors (Mori, 2002).

The relationship between L2 reading motivation and performance has also been investigated by some studies (e.g., Komiyama, 2009; Takase, 2007). The results are somewhat confusing and not conclusive; for example, Komiyama's study demonstrated that students with low motivational profiles had higher L2 reading performance. Takase's study found that there were no significant correlations between motivation and text comprehension. These results point to the need for further studies on these topics to explain them.

Takase's (2007) findings suggested that the relationships between L1 and L2 reading motivations were weak or non-significant. That is, motivated L1 readers are not necessarily motivated L2 readers.

The Gaps in the Literature

Recent research on L2 reading motivation has begun to shed light both on its nature and its role in developing L2 reading performance. Yet, compared to investigations into L1 reading motivation, much less research has been conducted in this area in L2 reading and further research is warranted. To be specific, several issues need to be addressed.

Limitations of the previous L2 studies include the fact that many components of L2 reading motivation that they identified require further validation. As an example, one of the major studies conducted by Mori (2002) has been criticized by Cho and Teo (2014) because they were unable to also identify five of the nine components she suggested in their own study.

Another limitation concerns the different nature of L1 and L2 reading. Most of the studies on L2 reading motivation have used the L1 reading motivation questionnaire developed by Wigfield and Guthrie (1997). In that questionnaire, competition in reading, reading recognition, and reading for grades were categorized as the components of extrinsic motivation for reading. However, it is anticipated that different types of extrinsic components may emerge in L2 reading. Attempting to take account of expected differences, for example, Mori's study (2002) also added 'integrative orientation' as a possible component of extrinsic motivation for L2 reading; however, this component failed to emerge. The current study suggested that 'instrumental orientation' (Gardner,1985) instead of 'integrative motivation', for L2 reading be included as one of the extrinsic components because the research was done in Japan where English is valued as an important tool for successful careers.

The sample size is also seen as a limitation because the numbers of participants were relatively small. Furthermore, because the major studies conducted have dealt with only female students or particular groups of students attending one college or one high school (Mori, 2002; Takase, 2007), it is difficult to generalize the results of the studies to other Japanese college learners. Thus, larger scale studies involving both male and female students attending different universities need to be conducted.

In addition to these limitations, some gaps in the previous research need to be addressed. One of these arises from a few studies that have examined the relationship between L1 and L2 reading motivation. It has often been assumed that if individuals are motivated to read in their

L1, this motivation will transfer to reading in L2. However, one study (Takase, 2007) has found that L1 and L2 reading motivations were not significantly related. This study, too, needs to be repeated with a larger group of learners and include both genders.

Purposes of the Study and Research Questions

The current study was motived by three purposes. The first purpose was to examine the multi-dimensional motivational components influencing Japanese college learners reading in L2. The theoretical framework of the study includes expectancy-value theory (Eccles, 1983), self-determination theory (Deci & Ryan, 1985a), instrumental orientation (Gardner, 1985), and self-confidence theory (Clement & Kruidenier, 1985).

The research questions that guided the study are as follows:
1. What are the components of Japanese college learners' motivation for L2 reading?
2. What are the relationships between L2 reading motivation and its components?

In summary, the studies conducted on L2 reading motivation have contributed to understanding of the nature of L2 reading motivation; however, because the number of the studies is still limited, and the results require further validation. Further studies on the exact nature of L2 reading motivation should be conducted.

CHAPTER 4
METHODS

In this chapter the methodology used in this cross-sectional study is presented. After the participants are described, the instruments, procedures, data preparation and analyses used in the current study are explained.

Participants

The participants in the cross-sectional study were 1,030 Japanese students enrolled in nine colleges (one public and eight private colleges) in the Kanto and Tohoku regions in Japan. In order to obtain data from a reasonably diverse sample of students, a variety of majors from different types of educational institutions was selected. These included music, liberal arts, English language and literature, economics, environmental studies, commerce, and international studies. Eight colleges were coeducational, and one was a women's college in the Kanto region. Hereafter, these colleges will be referred to as College A, College B, College C, College D, College E, College F, College G, College H, and College I.

Three of the colleges had high rankings, based on their difficulty of entry (Colleges C, D, and F). Colleges B, E, H, and I were considered average, and Colleges A and H were low. The degrees of difficulty of entry to these universities are indicated in Table 13, using *hensachi*, standardized scores published by one of the major preparatory schools for college entrance examinations (Kawai Jyuku Educational Information Network, 2011). The scores cover a wide range from the highest at 67.5 to the lowest at 35. (The average is 50).

Eight of the universities offered one or two English classes as part of the general education curriculum (*Ippan Kyōyō*) while Colleges C and F offered an intensive English curriculum where the first- and second-year students were required to take several academic English classes. The number of participants from each college ranged from 23 (College I) to 408 (College A) (Table 5).

The majority of the participants were first-year students ($n = 870$, 84.4%) while the rest were in their second year ($n = 160$, 15.6%). Their ages ranged from 18 to 21 years old. The male-female ratio was 36.6% ($n = 377$) for males and 60.9% ($n = 619$) for females (gender unknown = 2.5%, $n = 34$). All of them had studied English for a minimum of six years at junior and senior high school in Japan before entering their respective colleges.

For the cross-sectional study, the data were collected without names; therefore, consent forms were not distributed except for one college where they were required by administrators. However, basic ethical issues were explained to the participants by their teachers, who administered the questionnaire. The participants were told that they had the right to refuse to answer any items on the questionnaire and that their responses would be kept anonymous.

Table 5. *The Participants*

College	*Hensachi*	Year	*n* (Male/Female)	Major
A	35.0	1-2	400 (63/337)	Music
B	50.0	1	282 (185/93)	Commerce
C	67.5	1	87 (24/35)	Liberal Arts
D	62.5	1	51 (9/39)	Liberal Arts
E	52.5	1	30 (14/16)	English Lang. & Lit.

F	62.5	1	23 (8/14)	International Studies
G	40.0	1	68 (54/15)	Environ. Studies
H	52.5	1-2	62 (21/41)	Economics
I	47.5	1	31 (0/31)	English Lang. & Lit.

Note. N = 1,030 (Male students = 377, Female students = 619, Gender unknown = 34). The *hensachi* scores were drawn from Kawai Jyuku Educational Information Network (2011). All colleges were private except for D.

Instrumentation

A questionnaire was used to measure L2 learners' reading motivation in the study: a reading motivation questionnaire. The construction of the instrument is described in the next section.

The Reading Motivation Questionnaire

The Reading Motivation Questionnaire (RMQ) consisted of 69 items designed to measure nine constructs of L2 reading motivation. It consisted of two parts: 60 items designed to measure various aspects of L2 reading motivation and nine items designed to measure intrinsic motivation for L1 reading. The latter were added to investigate any connection between L1 and L2 reading motivation.

Most of the constructs measured on the questionnaire were drawn from Wang & Guthrie's L1 reading motivation questionnaire (2004) and some items were added from the questionnaires written by Mori (2002) and Takase (2007). 'Instrumental orientation' was added because it was assumed that L2 university learners often read L2 reading materials for such instrumental purposes as taking tests, doing assignments, getting a job or studying abroad. L2 Reading Self-Confidence (RSC) was added as well because self-confidence in L2 learning has been regarded as one of the most influential constructs that influence learning behavior (Clément, Dörnyei, & Noel, 1994).

In summary, L2 learners' reading motivation was hypothesized to consist of nine constructs, and five to nine questionnaire items were written to measure each construct: Curiosity (8 items), Involvement (8 items), Challenge (9 items), Recognition (6 items), Instrumental Orientation (6 items), Compliance (5 items), Importance (8 items), L2 Reading Self-Confidence (10 items), and Intrinsic Motivation for Reading in L1 (9 items). The 69 statements were randomly ordered. The participants responded to each statement on a four-point Likert scale (1 = *Strongly disagree*; 2 = *Disagree*; 3 = *Agree;* 4 = *Strongly agree*). The constructs with definitions and example items are listed in Table 6.

Table 6. *Constructs, Definitions and Examples of L2 Reading Motivation Questionnaire*

Constructs	Definition	Sample Item
Curiosity (CU) (8 items)	Desire to learn about a particular topic of personal interest	I want to read texts written in English.
Involvement (IN) (8 items)	Enjoyment of experiencing different kinds of literacy and informational texts	I often get deeply engaged when I read short stories written in English.
Challenge (CH) (9 items)	Satisfaction of mastering or assimilating complex ideas in text	Even though it is difficult to read novels in English, I'd like to try it.

Recognition (RC) (6 items)	Pleasure in receiving a tangible form of recognition for success in reading	I like to get compliments for my reading skills from my classmates.
Instrumental Orientation (INS) (6 items)	Belief that L2 reading is useful	I am learning to read in English because I want to get a job in which I can use English.
Compliance (CO) (5 items)	Reading because of an external goal or requirement	I read English because it is assigned as homework.
Importance of L2 Reading (IM) (8 items)	Belief that reading is an activity of central importance	Learning to read in English is important because it is useful for my future.
L2 Reading Self-Confidence (RSC) (9 items)	Belief that one is competent in reading.	I was good at reading English in senior high school.
Intrinsic Motivation for Reading in L1 (J) (9 items)	Fondness for and interest in reading in Japanese	I like reading books in Japanese.

Procedures

The data for the study were collected from the nine colleges over a three-year period. The participants spent approximately 20 minutes in their classes, answering the questions. The data were prepared for subsequent analyses by giving each case an ID number to indicate the school, the year of data collection, and each participant's gender. Then this information was entered into a Microsoft Excel 2010 (2010) spreadsheet.

Next, the Reading Motivation Questionnaire was reordered so that the items designed to measure the same constructs were together.

Analysis

Statistical analyses of the Reading Motivation Questionnaire occurred in two stages. First, a preliminary analysis of the questionnaire was conducted, using descriptive statistics to summarize the data and to screen them in preparation for the inferential statistical analyses. Second, an exploratory factor analysis was conducted to confirm the presence of the nine constructs. After these analyses, confirmatory factor analysis was carried out for each factor of L2 reading motivation. The purpose of this analysis was to investigate whether the items written for each factor formed unidimensional constructs. Through these preliminary analyses, 26 items of the questionnaire were removed. The remaining 46 items were submitted to the main analysis.

In this phase, the following statistical analyses were conducted. Exploratory factor analysis using Principal axis factoring with Promax rotation was conducted to answer the question concerning the identification of components of Japanese college learners' reading motivation. (Promax rotation was chosen because the hypothesized factors were expected to correlate with each other). Based on the results of the analysis, an L2 reading motivation model was constructed, and its validity and dimensionality were then tested by conducting confirmatory factor analysis with AMOS v21 (Arbuckle, 2012). Table 7 shows the summary of the analyses.

Table 7. *Research Questions, Variables, and Analysis*

Research questions	Variables	Analysis
1. What are the components of Japanese college learners' motivation for L2 reading?	Reading Motivation Questionnaire items	Exploratory factor analysis
2. What is the relationship between L2 reading motivation and its components?	Composite scores of the extracted factors	Confirmatory factor analysis

Chapter Summary

This current chapter has focused on the methodology used in the study, including information concerning the participants, instruments, procedures, data preparation, and statistical analyses applied to answer each of the two research questions. In the next chapter, the results of the first research question are reported.

CHAPTER 5
COMPONENTS OF L2 READING MOTIVATION

The purpose of this chapter is to report the results of the factor analysis of the reading motivation questionnaire. After the description of the principal components analysis, the results are discussed, referring to previous studies in L1 and L2 reading.

Results

The first research question was framed to identify the main motivational components of L2 reading. To answer this question, the responses to the L2 reading motivation questionnaire (RMQ) were examined, initially focusing on the factorability of the items. The Kaiser-Meyer-Olkin measure of sampling gave adequacy as .95, excellent for factor analysis (Field, 2009). Bartlett's test of sphericity was significant. However, two items had low communalities (CO_2 = .30 and J_3 = .26), so they were removed from the analysis. A principal components analysis was conducted with the remaining 44 items (see Appendix A and B for the final questionnaire in Japanese and English, respectively). Three criteria were used to determine the number of factors to rotate: the priori hypothesis, the scree test, and the interpretability of the factor solution. Based on these, eight factors were rotated, using a Promax rotation procedure which was chosen because the components were correlated (Tabachnick & Fidell, 2007).

The rotated solution yielded eight interpretable factors. Two items were deleted because they received lower loadings than .35 (Oshio, 2006). Although four items (CU2, RC1, CH1, and CH3) loaded on two factors, they were kept in the analysis because the higher loadings of these pairs were above .49. For the remaining 42 items, Cronbach's alpha for each scale ranged from .78 to .90, all of which were satisfactory (Field, 2012). Altogether, the eight factors accounted for 65.19% of the variance. Table 8 summarizes the label given to each factor, number of items loaded on each factor, and the shared variance explained by each one.

Table 8. *Principle Component Analysis of the L2 RMQ*

Item	F1	F2	F3	F4	F5	F6	F7	F8
L2 Intrinsic (α = .90)								
IN3	.83							
IN2	.74							
CU2	.70							.34
CU4	.67							
IN4	.64							
IN5	.64							
CU9	.49							
Importance (α = .89)								
IM5		.90						
IM3		.88						
IM8		.76						
IM2		.76						
IM7		.70						
IM6		.68						
Compliance (α = .87)								
CO4			-.96					
CO1			-.94					

CO5	-.75				
CO3	-.54				
Confidence (α = .84)					
RSC2	.79				
RSC10	.75				
RSC5	.71				
RSC6	.62				
RSC9	.57				
L1 Intrinsic (α = .84)					
J2		.84			
J9		.79			
J5		.71			
J8		.63			
J7		.63			
Instrumental Orientation (α = .87)					
INS5			.93		
INS4			.84		
INS1			.63		
INS3			.58		
INS2			.56		
Recognition (α = .78)					
RC5				.80	
RC2				.80	
RC3				.64	
RC1	.32			.49	
Desire to Read (α = .89)					
CH1	.36				.75

CU1							.72
CH6							.66
CH3	.34						.49
CH5							.42
CH8							.39
Eigen.	13.99	3.66	3.02	2.62	1.69	1.56	1.28	.86
% of Var.	31.79	8.32	6.87	5.96	3.85	3.54	2.91	1.96
Var.								65.19

Note. IN = Involvement in L2 Reading, CU = Curiosity, IM = Importance of L2 Reading, CO = Compliance, J = Intrinsic Motivation for L1 Reading, RSC = L2 Reading Self-Confidence, INS = Instrumental Orientation, RC = Recognition, CH = Challenge.

Table 9 shows the descriptive statistics of the composite score, which is a mean score of the items that had their primary loading on that particular factor. Higher scores indicated greater degrees of motivation represented by each factor.

Table 9. *Descriptive Statistics of the Eight Factors of L2 RM*

Factor	M	SD	Skew.	Kurt.
1. L2 Intrinsic	1.97	.67	.53	.18
2. Importance	3.26	.58	-.94	1.60
3. Compliance	1.90	.67	.59	.26
4. Confidence	2.08	.65	.29	-.14
5. L1 Intrinsic	2.60	.72	-.15	-.49
6. Instrumental	2.31	.78	.23	-.59
7. Recognition	1.97	.68	.41	-.23
8. Desire to Read	2.61	.72	-.32	-.34

Notes. Responses were collected using a Likert scale, 1 = Strongly disagree, 2 = Disagree, 3 = Agree, and 4 = Strongly agree.

Table 10 shows the results of Pearson correlation coefficients among the eight factors.

Table 10. *Correlations Among the Eight Factors*

	F1	F2	F3	F4	F5	F6	F7
1. L2 Intrinsic	—						
2. Importance	.28**	—					
3. Compliance	-.32**	-.41**	—				
4. Confidence	**.67**	.28**	-.32**	—			
5. L2 Intrinsic	.28**	.14**	-.11**	.17**	—		
6. Instrumental	**.64**	**.46**	-.39**	**.52**	.17**	—	
7. Recognition	.21**	.24**	-.02	.22**	.03	.28**	—
8. Desire to Read	**.71**	**.55**	-**.57**	**.56**	.29**	**.64**	.25**

Note. The numbers in bold are large (> .50) or medium (> .30) correlations (Field, 2012). **p < .01

As Table 8 shows, the factor analysis yielded eight distinctive factors of L2 reading motivation. Factor 1 (α= .90) was composed of seven items. The strongest loading was from Item IN3 (*I often get deeply engaged when I read novels in English*). Three other comparable items (e.g., *I forget other things when I read novels in English*) which were all related to a state of deep involvement in L2 reading were Items IN2, IN4, and IN5. These items derived from an L1 intrinsic motivation factor, Involvement (Wigfield & Guthrie, 1985).

As well, three other items, which derived from another L1 intrinsic motivation factor, Curiosity (Wigfield & Guthrie, 1985), loaded onto the same factor. These items were related to fondness for reading L2 materials, (for example, Item CU2, *I like reading materials written in English*). This result indicated that involvement in L2 reading and love of L2 reading could be conceptualized as one factor because they are inherently intrinsic reading behavior. Consequently, this factor was labeled as L2 Intrinsic Motivation (hereafter, L2 Intrinsic).

Factor 2 (α= .89) comprised six items that loaded on to it significantly. The strongest item was Item 5 (*Learning to read in English is important because it will be conducive to my general education*). The other items, too, were related to intrinsic value in L2 reading. So factor 2, was labeled Importance.

Factor 3 (α= .87) was made up of four items, which were concerned with reading L2 texts because of the pressure from others or because of school requirements. The strongest was Item CO2 *(I reluctantly read English to satisfy course requirements)*. This factor was labeled Compliance.

Factor 4 (α= .84) consisted of six items, which were all related to perceptions of one's ability to read L2 materials. The strongest item was Item RSC2 (*I was able to read well in senior high school*). This factor was named as L2 Reading Confidence (hereafter, Confidence).

Factor 5 (α= .84) was composed of five items, all of which represented intrinsic interest in reading in the first language (L1), (for example, *I love reading books in L1* (Item J2)) and (*My hobby is reading books* (Item J9)). As a result, this factor was labeled L1 Intrinsic Motivation (hereafter, L1 Intrinsic).

Factor 6 (α= .87) was composed of five items, which were all related to the usefulness of L2 reading skills in one's future studies or careers, (for example, *I am learning to read in English because I might study abroad in the future* (Item INS5)). Therefore, this factor was labeled Instrumental Orientation (hereafter, Instrumental).

Factor 7 (α= .78) consisted of four items, which were concerned with one's desire to be recognized by others by performing well in L2 reading. The strongest item was Item RC 5 (*I want to read better to please my teacher*). This factor was named Recognition.

Factor 8 (α= .89) was made up of six items. The strongest item was Item CH1 (*Even though it is difficult to difficult to read novels written in English, I'd like to try it*). The second one was Item CU1 (*I want to read materials written in English*), which was related to the desire to read different types of reading materials in English. The other four items were Items CH1, CH6, CH3, CH5, and CH8 (e.g., Item CH3: *Even though it is difficult to read information written in English on the Internet, I'd like to try it*), which were also related to the desire to read English despite the difficulty of doing so. This factor, therefore, was labeled Desire to Read.

In summary, the results of the factor analysis showed that L2 reading motivation could be seen as being composed of eight factors (L2 Intrinsic, Importance, Compliance, L1 Intrinsic, Confidence, Instrumental, Recognition, and Desire to Read).

The Relationships among the Factors

As Table 10 indicated, many of the components were significantly and positively correlated. High and notable correlations are reported below. When interpreting the correlation coefficients, the following standards were applied: small > .10, medium > .30, large ≥ .50 (Field, 2009).

L2 Intrinsic was highly correlated with Desire to Read at .71, Confidence at .67, and Instrumental at .64 respectively, which indicated that intrinsic motivation, self-confidence, and self-determined types of external motivation (e.g., instrumental orientation) were closely connected. Importance was moderately correlated with Desire to Read at .55; however, its correlation with L2 Intrinsic was relatively low (.28).

L1 Intrinsic had low correlations with the other five components (L2 Intrinsic, Importance, Confidence, Instrumental, and Desire to Read, suggesting that L1 Intrinsic was more or less an independent factor that is unrelated to the other factors.

Recognition had weak correlations with five factors (Importance, Desire to Read, Confidence, L2 Intrinsic, and Instrumental), and non-significant correlations with L1 Intrinsic and Compliance. Compliance exhibited significant, but negative correlations with the other six components (Importance, Desire to Read, Confidence, L1 Intrinsic, L2 Intrinsic, and Instrumental).

In summary, these results suggested that self-determined types of factors (L2 Intrinsic, Desire to Read, and Instrumental) were closely related to each other while the other less self-determined factors (Compliance and Recognition) were relatively unrelated to the others. Furthermore, Confidence was closely related to the self-determined types of factors while L1 Intrinsic was only weakly related to them.

Discussion

The purpose of the first research question was to identify the main components of L2 reading motivation. The statistical analysis of the L2 Reading Motivation Questionnaire yielded eight components of L2 reading motivation described above. In the section below, these components are discussed, referring to previous studies in L1 and L2 reading motivation research.

Intrinsic and Extrinsic Motivations for L2 Reading

Previous research on L2 reading motivation has shown that it can be separated into two types: intrinsic and extrinsic. In an Asian context, Dhanapala (2008), for example, conducted a study with 123 Sri Lankan college students and 124 Japanese college students. She identified eight factors of L2 reading motivation, which were grouped into intrinsic motivation (Curiosity, Involvement, and Preference for Challenge) and extrinsic motivation (Recognition, Grades, Social Reading, Competition, and Compliance). In the US, Komiyama (2009) conducted a study with 2,018 students who were studying English in university/college language programs. Her findings suggested that L2 reading motivation consisted of eight factors of motivation, which also could be divided into intrinsic motivation (Curiosity, Involvement, and Preference for Challenge) and extrinsic motivation (Social Sharing, Competition, and Compliance). Consistent with these studies, the present study described here identified eight factors of L2 reading motivation, which could be categorized into intrinsic motivation (L2 Intrinsic, L1 Intrinsic, Desire to Read) and extrinsic motivation (Instrumental, Confidence, Importance, Recognition, and Compliance). Thus, the findings were consistent with these previous studies. This result seems to indicate that self-determination may potentially provide a most reliable framework for L2 reading motivation although further research is necessary.

Intrinsic Motivation for L2 Reading

The importance of intrinsic motivation in reading has been well acknowledged in the reading literature (Oldfather & Wigfield, 1996). If individuals feel that reading is inherently enjoyable and rewarding, they will voluntarily spend time on it. Csikszentmihalyi (1990) indicated intrinsic motivation to read leads to deeper engagement where readers often experience "flow", a condition where one is totally immersed in the act of reading, forgetting time passing by. The current study identified two factors of intrinsic motivation: L2 Intrinsic and Desire to Read.

L2 Intrinsic. L2 intrinsic consisted of two types of reading behavior: involvement in reading and love of reading L2 materials. Although these were separate factors in some L1 reading research (Wigfield & Guthrie, 1985), they formed one intrinsic factor in the current study. Additionally, with the highest loading (.86) of the eight factors, L2 Intrinsic was identified as pivotal to L2 Reading Motivation.

Despite its importance, the mean score of L2 Intrinsic was low at 1.96 (SD = .67) on the 4-point Likert scale (1 = *Strongly disagree*, 2 = *Disagree*, 3 = *Agree*, 4 = *Strongly agree*) (see Table 9). In short, many respondents disagreed with the statement that they were intrinsically motivated to read English. This result suggested that for many Japanese college students, intrinsic motivation to read English was low.

One of the possible causes of the low intrinsic motivation is that Japanese students generally have little experience in reading English for enjoyment or pleasure because they study English at school primarily for external purposes such as tests or entrance examinations. Although further investigations are required, this result seems to suggest the need to change the way English reading is taught in Japanese high school. To do so, it is necessary to investigate what kind of reading materials or teaching methods lead to higher intrinsic motivation for L2 reading. For example, it might be effective to incorporate extensive reading into the regular English curriculum because previous research has found that it is effective in fostering intrinsic motivation for L2 reading (Hayashi, 2008, 2011; Takase & Otsuki, 2012). These issues are revisited in the pedagogical implication section.

Desire to Read. Another factor which was categorized as intrinsic motivation for L2 reading is Desire to Read, which represented the feeling of wanting to read L2 reading materials despite difficulty. It exhibited the second highest standardized regression coefficient (.84), thus showing its important role in L2 reading motivation. In the current study, it correlated significantly and highly with L2 Intrinsic at .71; therefore, this factor was categorized as intrinsic motivation. However, it is important to note that it also significantly correlated with Instrumental, a self-determined type of extrinsic motivation, at .63. That is, Japanese students desire to read L2 materials not only to enjoy reading but also for practical purposes such as using their L2 reading skills for their future careers or studies. This result was not surprising because a second language is often learned to achieve external goals such as getting a good job or passing tests.

The mean score for Desire to Read was 2.60 (SD = .72). This score was slightly higher than the score for L2 Intrinsic; however, it was still lower than the median response (3 = *Agree*), so it was evident that many respondents' desire to read L2 materials was relatively low.

Extrinsic Motivation for L2 Reading

Along with the intrinsic motivation factors mentioned above, the current study identified four extrinsic motivation factors for L2 reading: Instrumental, Importance, Recognition, and Compliance. Each of these factors is discussed below.

Instrumental. Instrumental, which represents the desire to read L2 materials because L2 reading skills are useful, exhibited the third highest standardized regression coefficient (.74). Although this factor was not included in L1 reading motivation research, it was added to the present study because of its important role in learning L2 (Ur, 1996), especially in EFL contexts such as in Japan where English is regarded as one of the most valuable tools for successful careers and academic achievement.

This factor correlated significantly with L2 Intrinsic at .63 and Desire to Read at .63. Thus, this result suggested that those who have higher degrees of instrumental orientation for L2 reading tend to have greater intrinsic motivation to read in L2 and a greater desire to read L2 materials. In short, Instrumental is closely associated with intrinsic motivation. Furthermore, Instrumental had a moderate correlation with Confidence at .51. This indicated that those who wished to use English in their futures also had higher confidence in their ability to read English, perhaps reflecting a higher skill level.

The mean score of Instrumental was low at 2.30 with a higher standard deviation (SD = .77), which meant that there was wider variation in the desire to use English reading skills in the future. It might be possible to speculate that those with lower L2 reading ability felt that it was difficult for them to use the skills so they did not wish to use English them in their future. This was supported by the fact that Confidence was also low at 2.08 (SD = .65).

Importance. Importance represents individuals' perceptions of the value of and significance attached to L2 reading skills. L2 learners perceive L2 reading as important for a variety of reasons, including their future careers, academic achievement, and family and social expectations; therefore, this factor is influenced by both internal personal drives and external ones.

Importance received the fourth highest standardized regression coefficient (.54). Compared with the other factors described above, this coefficient was lower, showing that Importance had less influence on L2 Reading Motivation.

In L1 reading, Importance was regarded as an element of intrinsic motivation (Wigfield, 1997). However, in the current study, a different result emerged when the correlations with the other factors were examined. Importance was closely connected with Desire to Read at .55 and Instrumental at .46, but the correlation with L2 Intrinsic was much lower at .28. These results indicated that those who value L2 reading skills tend to desire to read and use the skills in their future lives, but that they might not be necessarily intrinsically interested in L2 reading. For this reason, Importance was categorized as one of the extrinsic motivation factors.

This finding indicated one noteworthy characteristic of Japanese learners of English. In EFL contexts such as Japan, proficiency in English is highly desired, and those who are proficient in it are socially valued and respected. As a result, Japanese students grow up with a strong sense that English skills are valuable and desirable. However, not everyone becomes a successful learner of English, and many do not acquire a good enough command of the language to read it fluently. Thus, it is possible for learners to value English highly, but they may not necessarily enjoy learning it.

The conclusion above is supported by the descriptive statistics as well. The mean score of Importance was the highest of the eight factors: $M = 3.25$ ($SD = .58$). Because the SD was lower than those of the other factors, this result can be interpreted to mean that most of the participants, regardless of their proficiency, agreed that L2 reading skills were important. In summary, although Importance was not a strong indicator of L2 Reading Motivation, it represented the participants' general perceptions of L2 reading. In other words, in Japan, while English reading skills are highly valued, this sense of value does not necessarily lead to intrinsic interest in L2 reading.

Recognition. Another extrinsic motivation factor, Recognition, exhibited the fifth highest standardized regression coefficient (.29), which was much lower than those of the other factors. The factor is related to the seeking of approval or respect from others (e.g., parents, peers or teachers) through demonstrating good L2 reading performance. Because it focuses on others' perceptions, the perceived locus of causality is entirely external, compared with the two extrinsic factors described above (Instrumental and Importance). Naturally, Recognition had low correlations with Instrumental Orientation (.27), Desire to Read (.25), Importance (.24), L2 Reading Confidence (.22), and L2 Intrinsic (.21) while the correlation with Compliance was non-significant. These results indicated, then, that Recognition was not an influential factor. This finding can be explained by the fact that the participants in this study were young adults who had already passed the entrance examinations to get into their respective colleges or universities. It appears that they were much less concerned about how their performance in L2 reading was perceived by others than the time when they were high school students.

Compliance. Compliance can be described as reading L2 materials as a result of external coercion or pressure. As has been stated earlier, this factor had significant but negative correlations with L2 Intrinsic (-.32), Desire to Read (-.57), Importance (-.41), and Instrumental (-.39). The mean score of this factor was 1.90 (SD = .67), which was the lowest of the eight factors. It appears that most of the participants denied the idea that they might read English because of pressure from others.

Thus, the study has identified four types of extrinsic motivation (Instrumental, Importance, Recognition, and Compliance). Among these four factors, Instrumental exerted most influence on L2 reading motivation while the even more external elements of motivation (Recognition and Compliance) exerted much less or negative influence. Furthermore, it was clear that the participants placed high value on L2 reading.

L2 Specific Factors

Two specific L2 factors, Confidence and L1 Intrinsic, were also identified as components of L2 reading motivation. When these two were compared, it was evident that Confidence had a much stronger connection with motivation to read than L1 Intrinsic. This result highlighted the difference between L1 and L2 reading motivation. It strongly suggested that even if learners are fond of reading in L1, they are unlikely to be motivated to read in L2 unless they have considerable confidence in their L2 reading ability.

Summary of the Findings

This chapter reported the results of the factor analysis and discussed the implications of each factor. Some of these factors derived from L1 reading motivation research, showing that L1 reading and L2 reading are inherently similar in many respects because both of them involve the reader, the text, and the interaction between them (Rumelhart, 1977; Singhal, 1998). This study, however, highlighted some differences between L1 and L2 reading because specific factors in L2 reading also emerged: Instrumental, Confidence, and L1 Intrinsic. In the next chapter, the creation of an L2 reading motivation model including these factors is described and discussed.

CHAPTER 6
L2 READING MOTIVATION MODEL

Using the eight factors of L2 reading motivation identified in the current study, an L2 reading motivation model was created. This chapter reports and discuss its validation processes and results.

L2 Reading Motivation Model

To address the second research question, "What are the relationships among the factors of L2 reading motivation?", the L2 reading motivation model was created, drawing on an L1 reading motivation study (Wang & Guthrie, 2004) as well as other motivation theories (mainly, self-determination theory, Deci & Ryan, 1985a). In addition, the correlation coefficients of the eight observed variables (Table 10) were considered. The dimensionality and validity of the model were tested, using confirmatory factor analysis (CFA) with asymptotic distribution-free (ADF) estimation in Amos v21 (Arbuckle, 2012). This estimation was chosen because the data showed evidence of multivariate kurtosis (Byrne, 2010). In order to make it easy to handle the data, composite scores (averages of questionnaire items loaded on each factor) were used, instead of the individual scores for each questionnaire item (Oshio, 2006). In the section below, the details of the model and its validation processes are described.

Creating the L2 Reading Motivation Model
The L2 Reading Motivation Model hypothesized that L2 reading motivation consisted of six observed variables (L2 Intrinsic, Desire to Read, Instrumental, Importance, Recognition, Compliance), which represented

different reasons why individuals want to read L2 materials. Unlike these, two variables of L2 reading motivation (L1 Intrinsic and Confidence) were considered to be pre-existing conditions for L2 reading motivation; therefore, they were placed as predictors of L2 reading motivation in the model (Figure 2).

As has been mentioned, these six variables of L2 reading motivation were classified into two groups (intrinsic and extrinsic) by consulting the correlation analysis (Table 10). The former included L2 Intrinsic and Desire to Read. The latter consisted of four different types of extrinsic motivation: Instrumental, Importance, Recognition, and Compliance. These six variables were placed in the model with the predictors described above.

Results

To examine the reliability and validity of the Reading Motivation Model (Figure 2), confirmatory factor analysis was conducted. Table 11 shows the summary of fit indices used in the analysis (Oshio, 2006).

Table 11. *Summary of Fit Indices Used in the Current Study*

Index	Significance
Chi-squared test	$p > .05$ good
Root mean square error of approximation (RMSEA)	$< .05$ good, $> .10$ poor
Comparative Fit Index (CFI)	$> .95$ good

Note. The chi-squared statistics were not used to assess goodness of fit because of the large sample size (Oshio, 2006).

The results indicated that all factors loaded significantly on the latent variable, L2 Reading Motivation, with loadings ranging from -.55 to .89. The Model, however, initially displayed poor fit, $\chi^2(20) = 484.36$, $p < .001$, CFI = .85, and RMSEA = .15 [90% CI = .14, .16]. Therefore, after modification indices were examined, paths that allowed error terms to covary were added one by one. In total, five paths were added. As a result, the fit indices improved to $\chi^2(14) = 125.52$, $p < .001$, CFI = .96, and RMSEA = .08 [90% CI = .07, 10]. The $\Delta\chi^2$ value was significant at 20.74. Given the significant improvement in overall fit, the L2 Reading Motivation Model (Figure 2) allowing the five error covariances was considered the model with the satisfactory fit indices (Oshio, 2006).

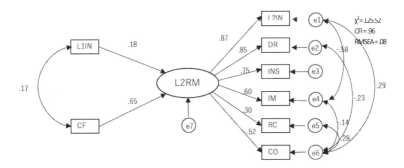

Figure 2. The L2 Reading Motivation Model.
L2RM = L2 Reading Motivation, L2IN = L2 Intrinsic, DR = Desire to Read, INS = Instrumental, IM = Importance, RC = Recognition, CO = Compliance, L1IN = L1 Intrinsic, CF = Confidence. N = 1024.

The L2 Reading Motivation Model demonstrated the strength of the relationships between the six observed variables and the latent variable, L2 Reading Motivation. The standardized regression coefficients ranged from .87 for L2 Intrinsic, .85 for Desire to Read, .75 for Instrumental, .60 for Important, .30 for Recognition, and -.52 for Compliance. This progression revealed that the higher the self-determination involved in each factor was, the higher the coefficient was: L2 Intrinsic was the highest and Compliance was the lowest.

The factor loadings of the predictor variables (Confidence and L1 Intrinsic) of L2 Reading Motivation indicated that Confidence was strongly related to L2 Reading Motivation at .65 whereas L1 Intrinsic was weakly related to it at .18. In other words, Confidence was an influential construct for L2 Reading Motivation while L1 Intrinsic was not.

To sum up, the L2 Reading Motivation Model demonstrated that L2 Reading Motivation is multifaceted, consisting of six motivational factors, which can be explained on the continuum of intrinsic and extrinsic motivation (Deci & Ryan, 1985). As the higher coefficients of autonomous types of motivation (L2 Intrinsic, Desire to Read, and Instrumental) indicated, it was evident that self-initiated motivation was more influential for L2 Reading Motivation than externally controlled motivation (Recognition and Compliance). Finally, the model showed that Confidence strongly affected L2 Reading Motivation, whereas L1 Intrinsic did not. These results are discussed below.

Discussion

The L2 Reading Motivation Model has shed light on several important aspects of L2 reading motivation. First, as has been noted earlier, L2 reading motivation is multifaceted, and elements can be divided into intrinsic and extrinsic categories (Dhanapala, 2006; Komiyama,

2013). The research makes it clear that Japanese college students read English for both intrinsic and extrinsic reasons.

Second, as the regression coefficients of the factors demonstrated, different factors influence L2 reading motivation according to how much self-determination is involved. The strongest influence comes from L2 Intrinsic, followed by Desire to Read, Instrumental, Importance, Recognition, and Compliance in that order. This finding agrees with similar results in L1 reading research where Intrinsic factors were found to have the greatest influence on reading motivation (Wang & Guthrie, 2004). At the same time, it is evident that an autonomous type of external motivation, instrumental orientation, plays an important role in L2 reading. Unlike first language, a second language is primarily learned to achieve external goals such as passing tests, getting jobs, or traveling overseas, so this finding is not surprising.

In addition, these findings provide support for a claim that self-determination theory can serve as a reliable theoretical framework for L2 reading motivation. As has been noted in Chapter 2 (Literature Review), this theory conceptualizes motivation as made up of different elements which can be placed on continuum, according to how much self-control is involved (Deci & Ryan, 1985). Similarly, this study demonstrated that the different factors motivating L2 reading were on a continuum of strength of influence decided by how much autonomy was inherent in each one.

Some may argue that instrumental orientation came from L2 motivation research (Gardner, 1985). However, some scholars have pointed out the similarity between instrumental orientation and identified regulation in self-determination theory (Heinzmann, 2013; Noel, 2001). The reason is that both of them are related to utility and value of activities in one's current and future lives. Within the framework of self-determination, identified regulation refers to a personal recognition of value in an activity because it is personally important (Ryan & Deci, 2000, p. 62). Instrumental orientation, similarly, refers to "the practical value and advantages of learning a new language" (Gardner & Lamber, 1972, p.132). Thus, it is clear that both of them are related to individuals' perceptions of value attached to an activity and that instrumental orientation and integrated orientation resemble to each other.

Third, the Model indicates that Confidence, with its high coefficient (.65), strongly predicts L2 Reading Motivation. In other words, if learners perceive their L2 reading ability as low, their motivation to read will also be low, but if they believe their second language skills are strong and their reading is easy and fluent, they will be more motivated to read second language texts. This can be corroborated by expectancy-value theory (Wigfield & Eccles, 1992), which suggests that unless learners have a prospect of success, they will not feel motivated to pursue the action.

Another possible predictor of L2 Reading Motivation was L1 Intrinsic; however, it was found to have only a weak relationship with L2 reading motivation (.18). This finding is noteworthy because only a few researchers have investigated the role of L1 intrinsic motivation in the field of L2 reading motivation. This study supports Takase's (2007) results, where she found that there was no significant relationship between L1 and L2 reading motivations. That is, those who read avidly in L1 were not necessarily avid readers in L2.

The relationship described above can be partially corroborated by the language threshold hypothesis (Cummins, 1979). That is, learners need to establish some knowledge of an L2 before they can successfully draw on their L1 reading ability (Bernhardt & Kamil, 1995; Lee & Schallert, 1997). In short, unless learners are proficient enough to understand L2 materials, they cannot utilize their L1 reading skills. Furthermore, if they do not understand the materials they read, they cannot enjoy reading and may not even try it.

Chapter Summary

The L2 Reading Motivation Model revealed several noteworthy aspects of L2 reading motivation. First, consistent with previous L1 and L2 research, both intrinsic and extrinsic types of motivation were identified.

The Model showed that high intrinsic motivation, as operationalized by L2 Intrinsic and Desire to Read, was a strong indicator of L2 reading motivation. Furthermore, it demonstrated that I instrumental orientation, a more autonomous type of extrinsic motivation, also strongly influenced L2 reading motivation. Third, it suggested L2 reading confidence exerted a strong influence on L2 reading motivation. If L2 learners perceive that their L2 reading is low, their L2 reading motivation is low and vice versa. Fourth, the model showed that less autonomous types of extrinsic motivation, were weak indicators of L2 reading motivation probably because the participants of the current study were young adults, not school children, who were more or less independent. Fifth, it demonstrates fondness for reading in L1 does not seem to transfer to L2 unless it is supported by L2 reading confidence. Unless learners have reached a certain level of L2 proficiency, they cannot utilize their L1 reading skills and resources, which, in a broad sense, might include motivation for reading.

Finally, these findings can be utilized to improve L2 reading instruction. This issue is discussed in the next chapter on pedagogical implications.

CHAPTER 7
PEDAGOGICAL IMPLICATIONS

Given the importance of motivation in reading (Wang & Guthrie, 2004), the current study investigated the components of L2 reading motivation. It is hoped its findings have shed light on the vital role of intrinsic motivation and autonomous types of extrinsic motivation in fostering motivation to read English.

In current college classrooms, especially in Japan, little attention is given to L2 learners' motivation to read in their second language. For example, the *Yakudoku* method, or the grammar-translation method, which basically consists of translation exercises, still persists in many English classes (Takase & Otsuki, 2012). In a typical class, one of the major activities is to translate English into Japanese. Whether or not such a class fosters motivation for reading English is questionable. Furthermore, a typical English textbook for Japanese college students consists of short passages, vocabulary lists, grammar exercises, and comprehension questions (Baba et al., 2015), and includes few interesting and engaging tasks or activities for motivational development. It seems that more attention paid to affective aspects of L2 readers by including different types of reading activities and materials would improve student interest and motivation. Several pedagogical suggestions are given below.

Fostering Intrinsic Motivation for L2 Reading

Considering the pivotal role of intrinsic motivation in L2 reading, reading activities that foster such motivation should be introduced. For example, research shows that extensive reading is effective for fostering fluency and interest (Day & Bamford, 1998) mainly for three reasons.

First, students are able to experience 'reading for pleasure' because reading materials for the extensive reading approach are often fiction, short stories or novels. So they can enjoy reading interesting and imaginative stories as they do in their first language. Second, materials for extensive reading are often graded readers, which are books that have had the language level modified to help L2 readers read them. Because students can choose a level appropriately matched to their L2 proficiency, they can understand the content without great effort and this may lead to increased confidence in their own reading ability. This confidence, in turn, may lead to an increased desire to read more. Third, in an extensive reading class, students are usually given the freedom to choose what they read and it becomes possible for them to choose content reflecting their own personal interests as well as lengthy enough text to develop fluency. In most programs, they are also given sufficient uninterrupted time to read to form a habit. In these ways, extensive reading may help students increase their intrinsic desire to read. Although an increasing number of educators have been practicing extensive reading in their classrooms, it should be practiced even more widely, including in junior and senior high schools and colleges as part of the regular curriculum.

Instrumental Orientation for L2 Reading

The study also found that instrumental orientation for reading was closely related to L2 reading motivation. That is, the more individuals desired to use L2 reading skills in their futures, the greater the motivation to read in L2 was. Because of this link, it makes sense for educators to increase L2 learners awareness of the usefulness and value of L2 reading skills in their future lives. One possible way for teachers to do this is to emphasize the fact that recently English has become a lingua franca, a common language between speakers whose native languages are different. Due to the acceleration of globalization, it has become possible to communicate in English in many countries around the world, although previously it used to be a language which was mainly used among native speakers of the language. It may also be useful to point out the value of English in many vocations and employment situations as part of career education. This kind of information may lead to heightened awareness of the utility of English reading skills and an increased desire to read L2 materials.

Self-Confidence in L2 Reading Ability

This study has found that self-confidence strongly influences L2 reading motivation. This is because expectancy for a successful performance is a prerequisite for the desire to perform an action (Wigfield & Eccles, 2002). Unless students expect that they can understand L2 materials, they are unlikely to even try reading them. Therefore, it is important for educators to help students feel more confident about their L2 reading ability. For instance, teachers can first use comprehensible materials at a child or student's own level, such as graded readers, children's literature, websites for children, or even their own transcribed writing, and then after students have more confidence about their reading performance, they can gradually introduce more challenging materials. Furthermore, teachers can model a variety of reading strategies such as chunking, inferencing, or summarizing to show how these can help with comprehension. In a small study conducted with less proficient college learners of English and using children's literature, the author found that, over a six-month intervention, students' self-confidence increased and so did their intrinsic motivation to read (2013). Although this was small-scale classroom-based research, it demonstrated the close connection between self-confidence and intrinsic motivation.

Content-Based Reading Instruction for L2 Classrooms

Content-Based Instruction (CBI) has been one approach to language teaching that focuses not only on the language itself but also on what is being taught through the language. The approach views the target language as "the vehicle through which a specific type of content is learned" rather than as the immediate object of the study (Brinton et al., 1989, p.5). For example, in an EAP (English for academic purposes) college context, students may study *Chinese history* with materials written in English, using English as the tool of study and communication. As a result, students are able to develop both their knowledge of the content and linguistic ability in English.

It has been widely acknowledged that content-based instruction can motivate L2 learners (Stryker & Leaver, 1997). When students have high interest in the content being taught, it is natural for them to become more engaged in learning the content even when it is taught in a second language. For example, if music majors read music related content in a college English class, it is likely that they become more interested in learning for two reasons. One, because they like music, it is interesting and engaging for them to read about it. Two, because they already have prior knowledge about music and this knowledge helps them understand the content even if reading in English is challenging. In addition, Grabe and Stroller (1997) argue that CBI classrooms generate increased motivation among students because "students are exposed to complex information and are involved in demanding activities which can lead to intrinsic motivation" (p. 20).

Concept Oriented Reading Instruction

Extensive research on reading motivation in L1 reading has resulted in one successful reading program, Concept Oriented Reading Instruction (CORI), which aims at fostering reading motivation and text comprehension (Swan, 2003). Because the present study has found that L1 and L2 reading motivations resemble each other to some extent, CORI may be an example of a program which could provide useful insights into L2 reading.

CORI is an instructional framework for content and reading instruction developed in the US during the last three decades. Based on extensive research on reading and educational psychology, CORI adopts an interdisciplinary approach by applying theories of motivation to content instruction in L1 settings (Guthrie & Wigfield, 1997; Swan, 2003; Wigfield & Guthrie, 1997). To date, this framework has been implemented in a number of schools in the US, including elementary schools, middle schools, and colleges, and it has demonstrated a significant impact in improving L1 learners' reading comprehension, motivation for reading, and conceptual knowledge (Guthrie, McRae & Klauda, 2009).

CORI systematically incorporates both cognitive and affective aspects of reading into academic content instruction. A typical CORI lesson consists of three strands of instruction: strategy instruction, academic content such as math, history, or science, and motivational support, all of which are carefully interwoven in a curriculum design. For example, in a science class in elementary school, students learn about "stars" by reading a variety of books while learning how to use reading strategies such as inferencing, predicting, or finding the main idea. During the process, motivational support such as "choice", "confidence support", or "collaboration" are carefully built into the activities.

The central goal of CORI is to increase students' reading comprehension by enhancing their reading engagement, which can be defined as "a construct that fuses motivational, cognitive, and behavioral attributes of students" (Guthrie, McRae, & Klauda, 2007, p. 238). In brief, engaged readers are internally motivated to read; they actively use cognitive strategies to link their old knowledge to new information gained from reading; they display active participation, effort, and persistence in the face of difficulty; they interact positively with other readers in classrooms; and they often read for pleasure as well as for learning. In sum, engaged readers are motivated, knowledgeable, strategic, and socially active. Thus, CORI aims to provide optimal conditions to lead to deep engagement during reading. Although L1 reading and L2 reading differ in many respects, some valuable insights can be gained from this program. It may well be worth adapting such practices as CORI encourages to L2 reading.

Chapter Summary

The chapter described some pedagogical suggestions for fostering motivation for L2 reading based on the findings of the study. Despite the important role of L2 reading motivation in L2 reading, little attention has currently been given to it. It is hoped that the study described in this book has provided some useful information to improve L2 reading pedagogy.

CHAPTER 8
CONCLUSION

In this chapter, a brief summary of the findings is presented, followed by a discussion of the limitations of the study and by suggestions for future research topics. Finally, concluding comments are given.

Summary of the Findings

The study presented in this book investigated Japanese college students' motivation for reading English. Its findings confirmed the multifaceted nature of L2 reading motivation, which is made up of intrinsic and extrinsic components (L2 Intrinsic, Desire to read, Instrumental Orientation, Importance, Recognition, and Compliance). These components were explained, referring to previous studies in L1 and L2 reading.

The present study suggested intrinsic motivation and instrumental orientation were highly influential for L2 reading motivation and that, compared to these factors, less autonomous types of extrinsic motivation (Recognition and Compliance) were much less influential. These findings appear to support the idea that self-determination theory (Deci & Ryan, 1985) aptly provides a comprehensible framework for L2 reading motivation.

The suggested L2 reading motivation model demonstrated relationships between the components and L2 reading motivation. Two predictors of L2 motivation (Confidence and L1 Intrinsic) showed that the former was a much stronger predictor of L2 reading motivation than the latter. This means that if individuals perceived that their L2 reading skills were high, their L2 reading motivation was also high. However, individuals' love of reading in the L1 had a much weaker connection with

L2 reading motivation. This finding confirmed the importance of L2 linguistic ability in L2 reading because no matter how much learners love reading in their first language, this love needs to be supported by their L2 proficiency in order to understand and enjoy what they read.

Similarities and differences between L1 and L2 reading motivations were confirmed. Five of the eight factors (L2 Intrinsic, Desire to Read, Importance, Recognition, and Compliance) were comparable to those discovered in L1 reading (Wigfield & Guthrie, 1995). In this way the findings indicated that L1 reading and L2 reading motivation share some similarities. However, the other three factors (Instrumental Orientation, L1 Intrinsic, and Confidence) were L2 specific factors. This finding points to the need for some practical implementations in reading programs, for example, giving explicit explanations to students as to why L2 reading is useful in their lives as well as providing enough support for the development of L2 reading skills to create confidence in reading.

Limitations

The present study is subject to several limitations that need to be addressed. First, it is a questionnaire study based on students' self-reports. The results from such a study do not necessarily provide deep insights into motivation to read in L2. It would have been better if the current study had also included a qualitative approach in the form of interviews or narratives. If students with extensive reading experience had been interviewed about how they perceived various aspects of L1 and L2 reading, that might also have been useful.

Second, the current study is a cross-sectional study which tends to show only limited aspects of the participants' affect. Thus the research design has an important limitation because motivation is a construct that develops and changes in response to both external and internal stimuli. It could have been better to have tracked longitudinal changes in L2 learners' motivation over one year or more.

The third limitation concerns the generalizability of the study. The number of the participants was large (N= 1,030), and they were from nine colleges in the Kanto and Tohoku regions. However, their majors were limited to liberal arts, commerce, English, environmental studies, and music. If students with a wider variety of majors had participated in the study, it is possible tjathe results might have been different.

The last limitation concerns the items written for the L2 reading motivation questionnaire. In recent years, Japanese university students spend more and more time reading information on the Internet; therefore, if some questionnaire items had specifically been written to investigate the factors behind this motivation to read, different constructs might have emerged as factors in L2 reading motivation.

Suggestions for Future Research

Further research needs to be conducted to explore the role of L2 reading motivation in L2 reading comprehension. Hopefully, this would lead to enhanced motivation and improved L2 reading instruction.

First, a replication study should be conducted with learners with a wider variety of majors. The findings might reveal that L2 reading motivation differs, depending on the learners' academic interests and L2 achievement. Furthermore, it would be useful to investigate what kind of L2 reading experiences L2 learners have had before entering college. For example, those who engaged in extensive reading in high school might show different profiles from those who did not.

Second, it would be useful to investigate what kind of L2 reading materials would enhance motivation to read. For example, it would be worth investigating the effects of using online materials on L2 learners' desire to read. In recent years, learners often study English using the Internet. *TED Conference,* for example, provides popular materials. Although TED Talks are aimed at native speakers, learners can study English by watching the talk videos and reading the subtitles at the same time. Materials learners can watch, listen to, and read increase learning effects and the use of such innovative media are worth exploring.

A third suggestion for future research concerns L2 reading instruction. Traditionally, L2 reading instruction has mainly focused on cognitive aspects of reading such as vocabulary, syntax, memory, and schema. However, as is stated in the pedagogical implication section, an integrated reading instruction program which incorporates both cognitive and affective components should be created and tested, perhaps borrowing from successful instruction programs like Concept Oriented Reading Instruction in L1 reading.

Final Conclusion

The findings of the study reported here have shed some light on Japanese learners' motivation for reading English. It is hoped that the study will serve as a partial foundation for creating a better understanding of how to foster L2 learners' motivation to read and how to improve their reading instruction. Hopefully, the study has also provided useful information on which to base the further research that is needed.

REFERENCES

Arbuckle, J. I. (2012). Amos (Version 21.0). Chicago: SPSS Inc.

Baba, C., Hayashi, C., Nakaya, M., Yukita, M., & Sugita, C. (2015). *The Analysis of English Textbooks for Remedial Learners of English*. Poster presented at the JACET International Conference, Kagoshima.

Baker, L., Afflerbach, P., & Reinking, D. (1996). Developing engaged readers in school and home communities: An overview. In L. Baker, P. Afflerbach, & D. Reinking (Eds.), Developing engaged readers in school and home communities (pp. xiii-xxvii). Mahwah, NJ: Erlbaum.

Baker, L., & Wigfield, A. (1999). Dimensions of children's motivation for reading and their relations to reading activity and reading achievement. *Reading Research Quarterly, 34,* 452-477.

Bandura, A. (1997). *Self-efficacy: The exercise of control*. New York, NY: W. H. Freeman.

Bandura, A. (1986). Social foundations of thought and action: A social cognitive theory. Upper Saddle River, NJ: Prentice Hall.

Bandura, A. (2004). Swimming against the mainstream: The early years from chilly tributary to transformative mainstream. Behavior Research and Therapy, 42, 613-630.

Bernhardt, E., & Kamil, M. (1995). Interpreting relationships between L1 and L2 reading: Consolidating the linguistica threshold and the linguistic interdependence hypotheses. *Applied Linguistics, 16*(1), 15-34.

Brinton, D., Snow, M., & Wesche, M. (1989). *Content-based second language instruction*. New York: Newbury House.

Byrne, B. (2010). *Structural equation modeling*. New York, NY: Routledge.

Cho, E., & Teo, A. (2014). Students' motivational orientations and attitude toward English learning: A study in the deep south of Thailand. *Asian Social Science, 10*(13), 46-54. doi:10.5539/ass.v10n13p46

Clément, R., Dörnyei, Z., & Noels, K. (1994). Motivation, self-confidence, and group cohesion in the foreign language classroom. *Language Learning, 44*(3), 417-448. doi:10.1111/j.1467-1770.1994.tb01113.x

Clément, R., Gardner, R. C., & Smythe, P.C. (1977). Motivational variables in second language acquisition: a study of Francophones learning English. *Canadian Journal of Behavioral Science, 9*, 123-133. doi.org.libproxy.temple.edu/10.1037/h0081614

Clément, R., & Kruidenier, G. B. (1985). Aptitude, attitude and motivation in second language proficiency: A test of Clément's model. *Journal of Language and Social Psychology, 4*, 21-37. doi:10.1111/1467-9922.53223

Cole, J. E. (2002). What motivates students to read? Four literacy personalities. *The Reader Teacher, 56*, 326-337.

Coddington, C. S., & Guthrie, J. T. (2009). Teacher and student perceptions of boys' and girls' reading motivation. *Reading Psychology, 30*, 225-249. doi:10.1080/02702710802275371.

Csikszentmihalyi, M. (1990). Literacy and intrinsic motivation. *Daedalus, 119*(2), 115-140.

Cummins, J. (1979). Linguistic interdependence and the development of bilingual children. *Review of Educational Research, 49*, 222-251.

Day, R. R., & Bamford, J. (1998). *Extensive reading in the second language classroom*. Cambridge, England: Cambridge University Press.

Deci, E. L., & Ryan, R. M. (1985a). *Intrinsic motivation and self-determination in human behavior*. New York, NY: Plenum.

Deci, E. L., & Ryan, R. M. (1985b). The general causality orientation scale: Self determination in personality. *Journal of Research in Personality, 19*, 109-134.

Deci, E. L., Vallerand, R. J., Pelletieir, L.C., & Ryan, R. M. (1991). Motivation and education: The self-determination perspective. *Educational Psychologist, 26*, 325-346.

Dhanapala, K. J. (2008). Motivation and L2 reading behaviors of university students in Japan and Sri Lanka. *Journal of International Development and Cooperation 14*(1), 1-11.

Dörnyei, Z. (2001). New themes and approaches in second language motivation research. *Annual Review of Applied Linguistics, 21,* 43-59.

Eccles, J. S. (1983). Expectancies, values and academic behaviors. In J. T. Spence (Ed.), *Achievement and achievement motives* (pp. 75-146). San Francisco, CA: Freeman.

Eccles, J. S., & Wigfield, A. (2002). Motivational beliefs, values and goals. *Annual Review of Psychology, 53,* 109-132.

Eccles, J. S., Wigfield, A., Harold, R., & Blumenfeld, P. B. (1993). Age and gender differences in children's self- and task perceptions during elementary school. *Child Development, 64,* 830-847. doi:10.1111/1467-8624.ep9308115032

Eccles, J. S., Wigfield, A., & Schiefele, U. (1998). Motivation to succeed. In N. Eisenberg (Ed.), *Handbook of child psychology: Volume 3--Social, emotional, and personality development* (5th ed.) (pp. 1017-1095). New York, NY: Wiley.

Elliot, A. J., & Church, M. (1997). A hierarchical model of approach and avoidance achievement motivation. *Journal of Personality and Social Psychology, 70,* 461-475.

Field, A. (2009). *Discovering statistics using SPSS.* London, England: Sage.

Gardner. R. C. (1985). *Social psychology and second language learning.* London, England: Edward Arnold.

Grabe, W. (2009). *Reading in a second language.* New York, NY: Cambridge University Press.

Grabe, W., & Stoller, L. F. (2002). *Teaching and researching reading.* London, England: Pearson Education.

Guthrie, J. T. (2001). Contexts for engagement and motivation in reading. *Reading Online, 4*(8). Retrieved from http://www.readingonline.org/articles/handbook/Guthrie/

Guthrie, J. T. (Ed.). (2008). *Engaging adolescents in reading*. Thousand Oaks, CA: Corwin Press.

Guthrie, J. T., & Alao, S. (1997). Designing contexts to increase motivation for reading. *Educational Psychologist, 32*, 95-105. doi:org.libproxy.temple.edu/10.1207/s15326985ep3202_4

Guthrie, J. T., & Alvermann, D. (Eds). (1999). *Engagement in reading: Processes, practices, and policy implications*. New York, NY: Teachers College Press.

Guthrie, J. T., & Davis, M. H. (2003). Motivating struggling readers in middle school through an engagement model of classroom practice. *Reading & Writing Quarterly, 19*, 59-85.

Guthrie, J. T., Hoa, W. T., Wigfield, A., Tonks, S. M., & Perencevich, K. C. (2006). From spark to fire: can situational interest lead to long-term reading motivation? *Reading Research and Instruction, 45*, 91-117. doi:org.libproxy.temple.edu/10.1080/19388070609558444

Guthrie, J. T., McGough, K., & Wigfield, A. (1994). *Measuring reading activity: An inventory* (Instructional Resource, No. 4). Athens, GA: National Reading Research Center.

Guthrie, J. T., McRae, A., & Klauda, S. L. (2007). Contributions of Concept-Oriented Reading Instruction to knowledge about interventions. *Educational Psychologist, 42*(4), 237–250.

Guthrie, J. T., Van Meter, P., McCann, A. D., Wigfield, A., Bennett, L., Poundstone, C. C., Rice, M. E., Faibisch, F. M., Hunt, B., & Mitchell, A. M. (1996). Growth of literacy engagement: Changes in motivations and strategies during concept-oriented reading instruction. *Reading Research Quarterly, 31*, 306-332. doi:org.libproxy.temple.edu/10.1598/RRQ.31.3.5

Guthrie, J. T., & Wigfield, A. (1997). Motivation for reading: An overview. *Educational Psychology, 32*, 282-313.

Guthrie, J. T., & Wigfield. A. (2000). Engagement and motivation in reading. In. M. L. Kamil, P. B. Mosenthal, P. D. Pearson, & R. Barr (Eds.), *Handbook of reading research* (3rd ed.) (pp. 403-422). New York, NY: Longman.

Guthrie, J. T., Wigfield, A., Metsala, J. L., & Cox, K. E. (1999). Motivational and cognitive predictors of text comprehension and reading amount. *Scientific Studies of Reading, 3*, 231-256.

doi: org.libproxy.temple.edu/10.1207/s1532799xssr0303_3

Guthrie, J. T., Wigfileld, A., & Perencevich, K. C. (Eds). (2004). *Motivating reading comprehension: Concept oriented reading instruction*. Mahwah, NJ: Erlbaum.

Guthrie, J. T., Wigfield, A., & Vonsecker, C. (2000). Effects of integrated instruction on motivation and strategy use in reading. *Journal of Educational Psychology, 92*, 331-341. doi:org.libproxy.temple.edu/10.1037/0022-0663.92.2.331

Hayashi. C. (2008). Short stories and cooperative learning in L2 reading classrooms. *The Journal of Engaged Pedagogy, 7*, 3-10.

Hayashi, C. (2010, August 3). *Extensive reading: Effects of different reading materials and styles on motivation to read*. Paper presented at the Japan Society of English Education (JASELE), Osaka.

Heinzmann, S. (2013). *Young Language Learners' Motivation and Attitudes*. London: Bloomsbury.

Jarvis, M. (2005). *The psychology of effective learning and teaching*. London, England: Nelson Thornes.

Jiang, X. (2011). The role of first language literacy and second language proficiency in second language reading comprehension. *The Reading Matrix, 11*(2), 177-190.

Kawai Jyuku Educational Information Network. (2011). 2012 Nendo-Nyushi-Jyouho（2012年度入試情報）.

Retrieved from http://www.keinet.ne.jp/doc/dnj/rank/index.html

Komiyama, R. (2009). Second language reading motivation of adult English-for-Academic-Purposes students. (Doctoral dissertation). Retrieved from Academic Premier.

Kowal, J., & Fortier, M. S. (1999). Motivational determinants of flow: Contributions from self-determination theory. *The Journal of Social Psychology, 139*(3), 355-368.

Lee, W., & Schallert, D. (1997). The relative contribution of L2 language proficiency and L1 reading ability to L2 reading performance: A test of the threshold hypothesis in an EFL context. *TESOL Quarterly, 31*(4), 713-739. doi:10.2307/3588007

Morgan, P., & Fuchs, D. (2007). Is There a Bidirectional Relationship between Children's Reading Skills and Reading Motivation? *Exceptional Children, 73*(2), 165-183. doi:10.1177/001440290707300203

Mori, S. (2002). Redefining motivation to read in a foreign language. *Reading in a Foreign Language, 14*(2), 91-110. Retrieved from http://nflrc.hawaii.edu/rfl/October2002/morimori.html

Mori, S. (2004). Significant predictors of the amount of reading by EFL learners in Japan. *Regional Language Centre Journal, 35*(1), 63-81.

Nishino, T. (2005). Japanese high school students' reading motivation. *Proceedings of the 4th Annual JALT Pan-SIG Conference.* Retrieved from http://jalt.org/pansig/2005/HTML/Nishino.htm

Noels, K. A. (2001). New orientations in language learning motivation: Towards a model of intrinsic, extrinsic and integrative orientations. In Z. Dörnyei & R. Schmidt (Eds.), Motivation and second language acquisition (pp. 43-68). Honolulu: University of Hawaii Second Language Teaching and Curriculum Center.

Oldfather, P., & Wigfield, A. (1996). Children's motivations for literary learning. In L. Baker, P. Afflervack, & D. Reinking (Eds.), *Developing engaged readers in school and home communities* (pp. 89-113). Mahwah, NJ: Erlbaum.

REFERENCES

Oshio, S. (2006). *Kenkyu-jirei de manabu SPSS to Amos niyoru shinri chosa kaiseki.* Tokyo: Tokyo-tosho.

Pajares, F. (1996). Self-efficacy beliefs in academic settings. *Review of Educational Research, 66,* 543-578. doi:10.3102/00346543066004543

Pintrich, P. R. (2003). A motivational science perspective on the role of student motivation in learning and teaching contexts. *Journal of Educational Psychology, 95,* 667-686. doi:10.1037/0022-0663.95.4.667

Pintrich P. R., & Schunk, D. H. (1996). *Motivation in education: Theory, research, and applications.* Englewood Cliffs, NJ: Merrill Prentice Hall.

Rumelhart, D. E. (1977). Toward an interactive model of reading. In S. Dornic (Ed.), *Attention and performance VI* (pp. 657-603). Hillsdale, NJ: Erlbaum.

Ryan, R. M., & Deci, E. L. (2000). Self-Determination Theory and the facilitation of intrinsic motivation, social development, and well-being. *American Psychologist, 55*(1), 68-78.

Schunk, D. H., Pintrich, P. R., & Meece, J. L. (2008). *Motivation in education.* Upper Saddle River, NJ: Pearson.

Singhal, M. (1998). A comparison of L1 and L2 reading: Cultural differences and schema. *The Internet TESL Journal, Vol. IV, 10.* Retrieved from http://iteslj.org/Articles/Singhaal-ReadingL1L2.html

Stryker, S. & Leaver, B. (1997). *Content-based instruction in foreign language education: models and methods.* Washington D.C.: Georgetown University Press.

Swan, E. A. (2003). *Concept-oriented reading instruction: Engaging classrooms, lifelong learners.* New York, NY: Guilford Press.

Tabachnik, B. G., & Fidell, L. S. (2007). *Using multivariate statistics.* Boston, MA: Pearson Education.

Takase, A. (2007). Japanese high school students' motivation for extensive L2 reading. *Reading in a Foreign Language 19*(1), April 2007, 1-17. Retrieved from http://nflrc.hawaii.edu/rfl/april2007/takase/takase.html

Takase, A., & Otuki, K. (2012). New challenges to motivate remedial EFL students to read extensively. *Journal of Applied Language Studies, 6*(2), 75-94.

Torgesen, J.K., Houston, D.D., Rissman, L.M. ,Decker, S.M., Roberts, G., Vaughn, S., Wexler, J., Francis, D.J., & Rivera, M.O. (2007). *Academic literacy instruction for adolescents: A guidance document from the Center on Instruction.* Center on Instruction for K-12 Reading, Math, and Science. Portsmouth, NH.

Ur, P. (1996). *A course in language teaching: Practice and theory.* Cambridge: Cambridge University Press.

Wang, J. H., & Guthrie, J. T., (2004). Modeling the effects of intrinsic motivation, extrinsic motivation, amount of reading, and past reading achievement on text comprehension between U.S. and Chinese students. *Reading Research Quarterly, 39,* 162-186.

Warden, C. A., & Hsui, J. L. (2000). Existence of integrative motivation in an EFL setting. Foreign Language Annals, 33(5), 547-555.

Wigfield, A. (1994). Expectancy-value theory of achievement motivation: A developmental perspective. *Educational Psychology Review, 6,* 49-78.

Wigfield, A. (1997). Reading motivation: A domain-specific approach to motivation. *Educational Psychologist, 32,* 59-68.
doi:org.libproxy.temple.edu/10.1207/s15326985ep3202_1

Wigfield, A. (2000). Facilitating children's reading motivation. In L. Baker, M. Dreher, & J. T. Guthrie (Eds.), *Engaging young readers: Promoting achievement and motivation* (pp. 140-58). New York, NY: Gilford.

Wigfield, A., Byrnes, J. P., & Eccles, J. S. (2006). Development during early and middle adolescence. In P. A. Alexander & P. H. Winnie (Eds.), *Handbook of educational psychology* (2nd ed., pp. 87-113). Mahwah, NJ: Erlbaum.

Wigfield, A., & Eccles, J. S. (1992). The development of achievement task values: A theoretical analysis. *Developmental Review, 12,* 265-310.
doi:org.libproxy.temple.edu/10.1016/0273-2297(92)90011-P

REFERENCES

Wigfield, A., & Eccles, J. S. (2000). Expectancy-value theory of achievement motivation. *Contemporary Educational Psychology, 25*, 68-81. doi:10.1006/ceps.1999.1015

Wigfield, A., & Eccles, J. S. (Eds.) (2002). *Development of achievement motivation.* San Diego, CA: Academic Press.

Wigfield, A., & Guthrie, J. T. (1995). *Dimensions of children's motivations for reading: An initial study* (Research Rep. No. 34). Athens, GA: National Reading Research Center.

Wigfield, A., & Guthrie, J. T. (1997). Relations of children's motivation for reading to the amount and breadth of their reading. *Journal of Educational Psychology, 89*, 420-432. doi:org.libproxy.temple.edu/10.1037/0022-0663.89.3.420

Wigfield, A., & Guthrie, J. T. (2010). The impact of concept-oriented reading instruction on students' reading motivation, reading engagement, and reading comprehension. In J. L. Meece & J. S. Eccles (Eds.), *Handbook of research on schools, schooling, and human development* (pp. 463-477). Mahwah, NJ: Erlbaum.

Wigfield, A., Guthrie, J. T., & McGough, K. (1996). *A questionnaire measure of reading motivation* (Instructional Resource No. 22). Athens, GA: National Reading Research Center.

Wigfield, A., Wilde, K., Baker, L., Fernandez-Fein, S., & Scher, D. (1996). *The nature of children's reading motivation, and their relations to reading frequency and reading performance* (Reading Research Rep. No. 63). Athens, GA: National Research Center.

Zimmerman, B. J., & Schunk, D. H. (2008). Motivation: An essential dimension of self-regulated learning. In D. H. Schunk & B. J. Zimmerman (Eds.), *Motivation and self-regulated learning* (pp. 1-30). New York, NY: Routledge.

APPENDIX A

THE FINAL L2 READING MOTIVATION QUESTIONNAIRE (JAPANESE)

1	CU1	英語で書かれた小説を読みたい。
2	CU2	英語で書かれた小説を読むのが好きだ。
3	CU4	英語で書かれた新聞を読むのが好きだ。
4	CU9	授業外でも英語を読むのが好きだ。
5	IN2	英語の小説を集中して読むことがある。
6	IN3	インターネットで英語で書かれた情報を集中して読むことがある
7	IN4	英語で書かれた面白いお話を読んで、他のことを忘れることがある。
8	IN5	英語で書かれた面白いお話を読んで、時間が経つのを忘れることがある。
9	CH1	英語の小説を読むことは、難しくてもやってみたい。
10	CH3	英語の情報をインターネットで読むことは、難しくてもやってみたい。
11	CH5	英文を読んで、英語を理解するのが好きだ。
12	CH6	難しい単語や表現があっても、英文を読みたい。
13	CH8	難しい英文を読んで、英語力を伸ばしたい。
14	RC1	クラスメートから英語のリーディングがよくできるとほめられたい。
15	RC2	先生から英語のリーディングがよくできるとほめられたい。
16	RC3	親を喜ばせるために、英語の読解力をつけたい。
17	RC5	英語の先生を喜ばせるために、英語の読解力をつけたい。
18	INS1	英語を必要とする仕事に就きたいので、英語のリーディングの勉強をしている。
19	INS2	世界中のさまざまな人の考えを知りたいので、英語のリーディングを勉強している。
20	INS3	世界中のさまざまな文化を知りたいので、英語のリーディングを勉強している。
21	INS4	将来外国に住むかもしれないので、英語のリーディングを勉強している。
22	INS5	将来外国に留学するかもしれないので、英語のリーディングを勉強している。
23	CO1	英語のリーディングが宿題なので、仕方なく英語を読んでいる。
24	CO3	先生からのプレッシャーがあるので、仕方なく英語を読んでいる。
25	CO4	単位を取るために、仕方なく英語を読んでいる。
26	CO5	必修授業なので、仕方なく英語を読んでいる。
27	IM2	国際化時代に生きるためには、英語のリーディングは大事だと思う。
28	IM4	英語のリーディングは自分の視野を広げるために大事だと思う。

29	IM5	英語のリーディングは自分の教養を高めるために大事だと思う。
30	IM6	英語のリーディングは自分の知識を広げるために大事だと思う。
31	IM7	英語のリーディングは自分の英語力を高めるために大事だと思う。
32	IM8	英語のリーディングは自分の考える力を伸ばすために大事だと思う。
33	RSC2	高校で英語のリーディングは得意だった。
34	RSC5	クラスメートよりも英語が早く読める。
35	RSC6	英語をあまり日本語に訳さないで理解できる。
36	RSC9	少しくらい難しくても、読み進めていくうちに理解できることがよくある。
37	RSC10	英語の読解テストは得意だ。
38	J2	本（日本語）を読むのが好きだ。
39	J5	寝る前に、本（日本語）をよく読む。
40	J7	外出するときは、本を持ち歩く。
41	J8	おもしろい本（日本語）を読むと、やめられないことがある。
42	J9	お気に入りの作家がいる。

APPENDIX B

THE FINAL L2 READING MOTIVATION QUESTIONNAIRE (ENGLISH)

1	CU1	I want to read materials written in English.
2	CU2	I like reading materials written in English.
3	CU4	I like reading English newspapers.
4	CU9	I like reading materials written in English outside of the class.
5	IN2	I often get deeply engaged when I read English.
6	IN3	I often get deeply engaged when I read novels written in English.
7	IN4	I often get deeply engaged when I read information written in English on the Internet.
8	IN5	Once I start reading interesting text written in English, I lose track of time.
9	CH1	I enjoy the challenge of reading novels in English
10	CH3	I enjoy the challenge of reading information on the Internet in English.
11	CH5	I enjoy the challenge of understanding English when reading materials written in English.
12	CH6	I enjoy the challenge of trying to understand English passages even when I encounter difficult words or expressions.
13	CH8	I want to improve my reading abilities by reading more challenging materials.
14	RC1	I like to get compliments for my reading skills from my classmates.
15	RC2	I like to get compliments for my reading skills from my teacher.
16	RC3	I want to read better to please my parents.
17	RC5	I want to read better to please my teacher.
18	INS1	I am learning to read in English because I want to get a job in which I can use English.
19	INS2	I am learning to read in English because I want to learn about various opinions and views in the world.
20	INS3	I am learning to read in English because I want to learn about different cultures by reading English materials.
21	INS4	I am learning to read in English because I might live overseas in the future.
22	INS5	I am learning to read in English because I might study abroad in the future.
23	CO1	I reluctantly read English because it is assigned as homework.
24	CO3	I reluctantly read English because of pressure from my teacher.
25	CO4	I reluctantly read English to satisfy course requirements.
26	CO5	I reluctantly read English because English is a required course in my university. .
27	IM2	Learning to read in English is important because we are living in the international age.
28	IM4	Learning to read in English is important because it is useful for my future.
29	IM5	Learning to read in English is important because it will be conducive to my general education.

30	IM6	Learning to read in English is important because it will make me a more knowledgeable person.
31	IM7	Learning to read in English is important because it will develop my English abilities.
32	IM8	Learning to read in English is important because it will develop my thinking skills.
33	RSC2	I was able to read English well in senior high school.
34	RSC5	I can read English faster than most of my classmates.
35	RSC6	I can understand English without translating into Japanese.
36	RSC9	Even when I read difficult texts in English, I persist in reading.
37	RSC10	I am good at reading comprehension tests.
38	J2	I like reading books in Japanese.
39	J5	I often read Japanese books.
40	J7	I usually carry a Japanese book whenever I go out.
41	J8	When I read interesting stories in Japanese, I cannot stop reading.
42	J9	My hobby is reading books.